华 尔 街 英 语
南京市志愿者协会 编著

口袋里的西洋经

Wall Street English Appetizers: 123 Bite-sized Articles

南京出版传媒集团
南京出版社

图书在版编目（CIP）数据

口袋里的西洋经：汉英对照／华尔街英语，南京市志愿者协会编著. —南京：南京出版社

ISBN 978-7-5533-0755-8

Ⅰ.①口…　Ⅱ.①华…　②南　Ⅲ.①英语－自学参考资料　Ⅳ.①H31

中国版本图书馆CIP数据核字（2014）第272183号

书　　名　口袋里的西洋经
作　　者　华尔街英语，南京市志愿者协会
出版发行　南京出版传媒集团
　　　　　　南　京　出　版　社

社址：南京市太平门街53号　　　邮编：210016
网址：http://www.njcbs.cn　　　淘宝网店：http://njpress.taobao.com
联系电话：025-83283871、83283864（营销）　025-83112257（编务）

出 版 人　朱同芳
责任编辑　谢　微
装帧设计　王　敏
责任印制　杨福彬

排　　版　南京新华丰制版有限公司
印　　刷　南京玉河印刷厂
开　　本　787毫米×1092毫米　1/32
印　　张　5.75
字　　数　100千字
版　　次　2015年3月第1版
印　　次　2015年3月第1次印刷
书　　号　ISBN　978-7-5533-0755-8
定　　价　26.00元

营销分类：英语学习

编委会

Foreword

This is a collection of our favorite short articles written by twelve Wall Street English foreign teachers for people interested in practicing their English. With six chapters and many topics, there will be something of interest to everyone!

前　言

这是一本由12位来自华尔街英语的资深外教原创的英语休闲短文集锦。文章短小精悍，通俗易懂，为广大英语学习爱好者量身打造。本书包含了六个章节，话题内容丰富广泛，希望您能喜爱并能够从中获益。

Author's Note

This is more than a book about English. It has something we can all relate to - life, culture, business, hobbies, holidays and so on. Its various authors approach subjects from different angles due to their varying interests, opinions and writing styles, thus creating a more dynamic book about English. It hands down a light, enjoyable read for everyone!

Heather Pfeiffer

这不仅仅是一本关于英语的书，它的内容涉及生活、文化、商务，爱好、度假等方方面面。每个作者从自己的兴趣出发，各抒己见，用多彩的写作风格、从不同角度探讨一个个生动有趣的话题，从而打造出一本更为生动的英语书。信手翻阅，享受阅读吧！

Greetings Readers!

I applaud you for continuing to improve your English skills! Every day that you learn a new vocabulary word or a new grammar point is a day of improvement in your English proficiency, and that is something you can always be proud of!

As a foreign language student myself, I know that studying English can be frustrating at times. I know that sometimes you feel like you are not making any progress at all, and that can be very discouraging. But I assure you that you ARE making progress. I promise you! You just don't see it. As long as you are studying a little bit of English each day, you ARE improving, and one day, you will suddenly realize, "Whoah, my English is awesome!"

Mann Monroe, Esq, MBA

roe@monroemann.com

WeChat:MonroeMann

首先，恭喜你的英文水平日益精进！每天，当你学会一个英文单词或者一个新的语法知识时，你都在不断提高你的英文水平，这会让你很有成就感！

作为一名语言学习者，我知道英语学习有时候会令人沮丧。有时候，你会气馁地觉得你根本没有任何进步。但是我可以向你保证，你其实一直在进步！只是没有注意到罢了。只要每天坚持不懈地学习点英语，英语水平就会不断提高，然后，一天，你会惊然发现：“哇哦，我的英语已经变得超级棒！”

Table of Contents

Chapter 1　Wise Old Sayings　老话的智慧

Every culture has its own wise old sayings, pieces of wisdom which are handed down from father to son or mother to daughter. Learning wise old sayings can teach us to be wise, and help us to understand another culture. What can you learn from these?

每个国家或民族的文化里都包含着智慧的老话。处世的智慧由父亲传给儿子或由母亲传给女儿。学习这些智慧的老话能够让我们变得更加睿智，同时也可以帮助我们更好地理解其他文化。那么从这一章节你能学到什么呢？

The Early Bird Gets the Worm

Heather Pfeiffer

This is a useful phrase about success. Here is an example: Mary prepared for a business meeting in advance, thinking about any possible problems. John delayed preparing for the meeting and on the last day was still finishing last minute preparations. Who do you think was more successful? Exactly, Mary was the early bird who got the worm. "The early bird gets the worm" is a kind reminder to people that a person who prepares early in the day or early in a project and puts in effort is more likely to succeed.

早起的鸟儿有虫吃

这是一个关于成功的实用短语。例如：员工玛丽在会议前就提前做好准备工作，思考其他可能出现的问题。员工约翰在会前拖延工作并且在最后一天还在做最后一分钟的准备。你认为谁更会成功呢？显然，员工玛丽是早起的鸟儿，她能找到虫子吃。这个短语善意地提醒人们，提早做好准备并且用心付出努力更易获得成功。

Don't Count Your Chickens Before They Hatch

Lindsey Bard

The story is that a young girl was walking with a basket of eggs. She dreamed of when they would hatch into chickens and be sold, making her a lot of money. While she was walking she tripped, and all the eggs broke because she wasn't paying attention. "Don't count your chickens before they hatch", means don't just dream about your future plans, concentrate on what's happening now or your plans might never happen.

别高兴得太早

一个年轻的女孩儿挎着一篮鸡蛋走在路上。她梦想着鸡蛋都能孵出小鸡，然后拿去卖掉，再然后挣很多的钱。结果她一不留心被绊倒，结果所有的鸡蛋都摔碎了。“Don't count your chickens before they hatch”的意思是“别高兴得太早”。关注当下，不做白日梦，否则你可能一无所获。

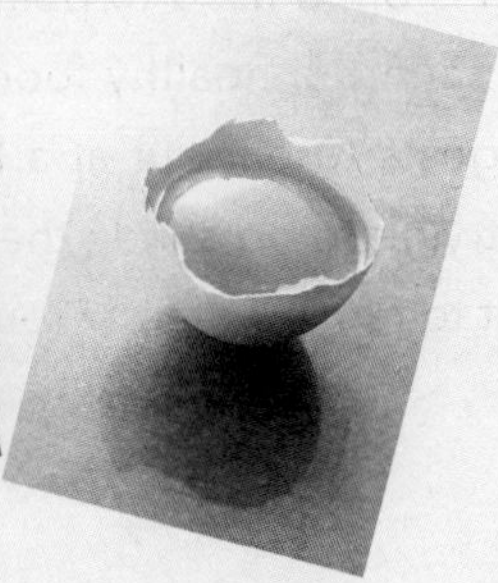

You Are What You Eat

Heather Pfeiffer

Do you consider yourself healthy? What do you usually eat? Would you rather eat out at a restaurant or cook at home? Have you ever heard the term"You are what you eat"? In other words, your health is connected to the food you put in your body. The term is often used to point out to someone that they are eating unhealthy food. So next time your friend suggests to eat out at a fast food restaurant, if you are trying to persuade them to eat healthier, you may want to remind them: "You are what you eat!"

吃什么像什么

你认为自己健康吗？你通常都吃什么？你是愿意在餐厅吃，还是在家里吃呢？有听过吃什么像什么的说法吗？换句话说，你的健康和你吃进身体的食物有关。这种表达方式通常用来告诫哪些正在吃着不健康食物的人。下次，如果你的朋友建议去快餐店吃，而你想劝他们吃得健康一些，你就可以提醒他们：吃什么像什么！

An Apple a Day Keeps the Doctor Away

Heather Pfeiffer

What do you usually eat for breakfast, lunch and dinner? Do you eat a healthy diet? When discussing health, English speakers might say this English proverb "An apple a day keeps the doctor away".It is used as a gentle reminder that eating healthy food prevents future ailments and sicknesses. If you want to encourage a natural healthy diet, you can say this. So next time when you are talking about health with a friend, you can playfully remind them to eat more apples.

一日一苹果，不用看医生

早餐、中餐、晚餐，你通常吃什么呢？你吃得健康吗？当谈论健康的时候，英语会话者会说一句英语谚语"An apple a day keeps the doctor away"，它被用来提醒人们吃健康的食物，预防疾病。如果你想要鼓励自然健康的饮食，你可以说这句话。因此，下次你和朋友谈论健康的时候，你可以半开玩笑地提醒他们要多吃苹果。

The Apple Never Falls Far from the Tree

Philip Simpson

Some things in life are unavoidable. You will die, you will pay tax, and there is a good chance you will end up like your mother or father. In fact, so many of us will follow closely to our parents that we have an expression for it in English. We say "the apple never falls far from the tree" which means that the fruit of a tree (you) will always be similar to what it came from (your parents). I made it to 26 before I started to notice my father's influence in myself...how about you?

苹果落地总是离树不远

一些事情是生活中无法避免的。你会死去，你要缴税，以及很有可能你最终的命运和你父母的惊人的相似。事实上，我们当中许多人将会跟我们的父母一样，过着相似的生活。于是在英语里就有了这样一种表达。我们说“苹果落地永远离树不远”，意思是，树上结出的果实（你），总是会与养育果实的大树（你的父母）相似。我注意到父亲对我的影响是在我26岁的时候，你呢?

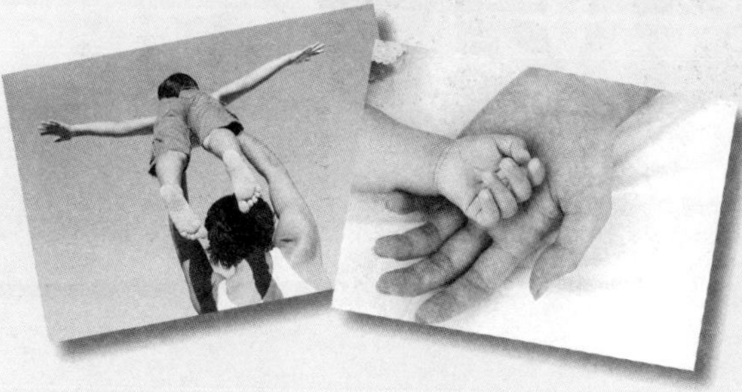

Curiosity Killed the Cat

Lindsey Bard

My cat found a box and tried to pull the lid up to see inside because she is curious. She got cut by the staple in the lid that she didn't see. "Curiosity killed the cat" is a reminder to be careful when trying new things, and to consider whether experimenting is really a good idea. Happily, my cat didn't die!

好奇心害死猫

我的猫咪找到一个盒子。出于好奇，它试着拉开盖子往里面看。结果它被盖子里没看到的订书钉割伤了。“好奇心害死猫”的意思是说，当你在尝试新事物时要小心谨慎，要考虑一下这样的尝试是否真的值得（管理好自己的好奇心）。幸运的是，我的猫并没有因此丢掉性命。

You Shouldn't Look a Gift Horse in the Mouth

Cher Reynolds

Before we had luxury items such as the Chanel bag or the iPad, giving expensive gifts was a very different story. Before the modern world as we know it people would impress their loved ones or clients by giving them a horse as a gift. This is perhaps the same as buying someone a new car. One way to check the health of a horse is to look inside its mouth, but to inspect a gift for its quality the second you receive it is considered bad manners; so we say "You shouldn't look a gift horse in the mouth".

别嫌东嫌西

在我们拥有像香奈尔包包或是苹果平板电脑这样的奢侈品之前，赠送的贵重礼物完全是另外一码事。在现代社会到来之前，据我们所知，人们通过赠送一匹马的方式来博取他们爱慕的人或客人的欢心。这或许跟在现在买一辆新车给某人一样。要检查马是否健康的一种方式就是看它的嘴。但是，在收到礼物时立刻检查礼物的质量，会被认为是不礼貌的行为。因此，我们会说“你不应该一收到礼物就检查，还嫌东嫌西的”。

It Takes Two to Tango

Philip Simpson

Latin dance has become very popular in China, with many young people deciding to take a sexy dance class instead of going to watch a movie. The tango is a dance that came from the northwest of Argentina, and is most famous for sometimes having dancers pass a rose from their mouth to their partners. "It takes two to tango" is a saying used to show that the blame for a bad situation should be shared by both people who took part. E.g:

Jim: His wife is always angry with him!

Sue: Well, it takes two to tango.

一个巴掌拍不响

拉丁舞在中国变得很流行。许多年轻人宁愿放弃看电影而去参加性感的舞蹈课。探戈是来自于阿根廷西北部的舞蹈，最出名的场景是舞者口含玫瑰并将它传递给其舞伴。"It takes two to tango"的意思是，如果因为两个人的共同参与而导致了一个困难状况的发生，那么这两个人都需要承担责任。比如：

吉姆说："他的妻子总是对他发脾气。"

苏答道："一个巴掌拍不响啊！"

Money Doesn't Grow on Trees!

Heather Pfeiffer

This is something parents love to say to their children. If money grew on trees, it would be very accessible. If I could find money in many places, I would use it without a second thought of worrying about regretting my purchase. Everyone would happily spend more money, right? (Naturally, this is if inflation also didn't exist.) So when someone says "money doesn't grow on trees", what they're really saying is that it's not easy to obtain money (so don't spend it carelessly).

钱不长在树上

这是父母们爱跟小孩们说的话："钱不长在树上。"如果金钱长在树上，那就很容易获得。意思是说如果我能在许多地方找到钱，我就能不假思索地任意挥霍钱财，并且不用担心因为花钱而产生负罪感。人人都愿意开心地花更多的钱，不是吗？（当然，假设通货膨胀并不存在。）因此，当某人说"钱不是长在树上"的时候，他们真正想表达的意思是：挣钱不容易（因此不要乱花钱）。

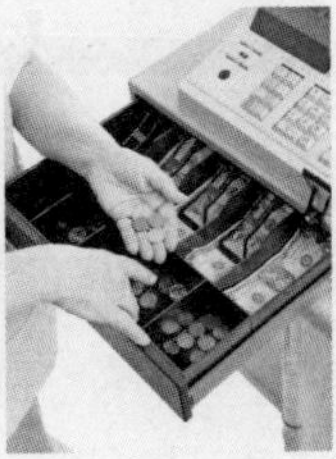

Don't Burn Any Bridges

Allen Mak

"Don't burn any bridges before you resign from your job." Have you ever heard of this phrase? The phrase means that we shouldn't destroy our relationship with our previous company or colleagues. The reason behind this is simple. If we keep a good, smooth, and strong relationship (the "bridge") then our ex-employer can give us a good reference for any future work opportunities. In the USA, employers always check their candidate's background information before hiring them. So we always tell each other not to burn any bridges.

别过河拆桥

"在你辞职之前，为自己留条后路。"你听过这样的短语吗？这个短语的意思是，我们不应该破坏跟以前公司和同事的关系。背后的原因很简单。如果我们保持良好、顺畅、强有力的关系（即所谓"桥"），那么我们的前雇主可以为我们未来的工作机会提供良好的证明。在美国，雇主总是在员工入职前核查求职者的背景信息。因此，人们总是互相告诫：不要过河拆桥。

The Grass Is Always Greener on the Other Side of the Fence

Allen Mak

Do you envy your neighbors? Do you always think that your neighbor's life is better than yours? As an easy-to-understand saying we often say "the grass is always greener on the other side of the fence". - meaning that your neighbor's garden, or house, or car etc. always looks better. But in reality you are just ignoring the negative items of your neighbor's life and downplaying the positives of your own life.

邻家芳草绿，隔岸风景好

你嫉妒你的邻居吗？你总觉得邻居生活得比你好吗？如果是这样，那么你可以用上这句很好理解的话：“邻家芳草绿，隔岸风景好。”即邻居的花园、洋房或者车，常常看起来更好。然而，在现实生活中，你却忽略了邻居的生活也并非事事顺心，而自己的生活其实也充满了积极的正能量。

美国的Neighborhood Watch（邻里守望相助）

Neighborhood Watch也称作“a crime watch”或者“neighborhood crime watch”，是指一种由邻里自发组织的预防犯罪以及破坏他人财物的组织。Neighborhood Watch的主要责任是邻里之间互相帮忙照看他人财物，看到形迹可疑的人及时报警。这种组织成立的主要目的是为了提高社区居民的安全意识，保护他们的生命和财产安全，同时增进邻里之间互帮互助的友好氛围。但前提是一定要保证自身的安全，发现犯罪最好报警而不要贸然采取干预行动。

When in Rome, Do As the Romans Do!

Tessa Xioutas

"When in Rome, do as the Romans do!" is an expression similar to "going with the flow" which means that you're doing something because everyone else around you is doing it. When you're visiting a new place you should try to act like the people from that place. This expression has also been shortened to "When in Rome!"

Bob: Let's go to KTV!

Mike: No thanks, I don't like to sing in front of people.

Bob: You should come! Shanghai has some great KTV places... "When in Rome!"

Mike: Oh okay, it could be fun!

入乡随俗

"当在罗马的时候，像罗马人一样做事"是一个和"入乡随俗"相似的表达。意思是，当你周围的人都在做某事时，你也要做同样的事情。当你参观一个新地方时，应该尽量像那里的人一样行事。这个表达可以简写为“When in Rome！”

鲍勃：我们去KTV吧！

麦克：不去了，谢谢，我不习惯当众唱歌。

鲍勃：你应该来参加，上海有很不错的卡拉OK厅……你应该入乡随俗！

麦克：好吧，那想来应该会很有意思！

Money Is the Root of All Evil

Allen Mak

Western countries have a common saying, "Money is the root of all evil". When I was young my mother taught me a very important lesson about money. She said: "The more money you want, the more foolish and uncontrolled desires you will have." It seems that my mother was correct. If we look at what caused the 2008 financial crisis, we can see the foolish and uncontrolled desires of the banks and of the ordinary citizens who over-borrowed. Everyone wanted easy money back then, and they made some foolish decisions. So beware you all, money is the root of evil and foolishness.

金钱是罪恶的根源

西方国家有一种说法，“金钱是罪恶的根源”。在我很小的时候，我的母亲就应如何对待金钱这一主题给我上了很重要的一课。她总说：“你越是想要金钱，你就会拥有越多愚蠢并且无法控制的欲望。”我妈妈说得似乎很对。如果看看2008年金融危机爆发的原因，我们可以看到银行以及那些过度借贷的人们的愚蠢且无法控制的欲望。那时，钱似乎都来得十分容易，人人都想赚快钱，（在金钱的驱使下）人们做了很多愚蠢的决定。因此，小心！金钱是罪恶和愚蠢的根源。

Seize the Day

Linda Napikoski

This phrase actually comes from the Latin "carpe diem". Its English meaning is "seize the day". To seize something means to take it while you have the opportunity. We say "seize the day" to encourage people to do their best and make each day of their lives special.

把握今天

这个短语实际源于拉丁语“carpe diem”。它的英文意思是“把握今天（seize the day）”。“To seize something”的意思是指当有机会的时候，你就要抓住。我们说“把握今天”来鼓励人们尽全力活出精彩的每一天。

Birds of a Feather Flock Together

Yusef Wateef

I don’t care if you are at work, at a friend’s house, or sitting with your family. Look at the person to your left, and to your right. If you can recognize them as winners, then you are probably a winner as well! Remember, "Birds of a feather flock together" !

物以类聚（相同羽毛的鸟会聚在一起）

我不管你现在是在办公场所，在朋友家里抑或是和家人在一起。看看你左边的那个人，然后再看看你右边的人。如果你认可对方是成功人士，那么极有可能你也是位成功人士。因为俗话说“物以类聚，人以群分”！

Pot Calling the Kettle Black

Lindsey Bard

"You know what your problem is?" my coworker asked me, "You talk too much." Then he spent the next five minutes telling me about how much I talk. A clear case of "the pot calling the kettle black". He was complaining about something I do that he also does.

五十步笑一百步（锅嫌壶黑）

“你知道你的问题是什么吗？”我的同事问我，“你讲话讲得太多。”接下来，他花了足足五分钟来告诉我我讲了多少话。这就是典型的“五十步笑一百步”，他抱怨的事情发生在我身上同样也发生在他自己身上。

Chapter 2 East Meets West 东方遇见西方

"East is East and West is West, and never the twain shall meet." said Author Rudyard Kipling. In 1889, Rudyard Kipling wrote about how the culture of the east and the west could never meet in the middle. What would he think if he could see the modern world?

英国作家鲁迪亚德·吉卜林曾说过："东方是东方，西方是西方，两者永不相会。"1889年，他发表了一些关于西方文化和东方文化永远不会相互融合的文章。如果他能活到现在，看到当今的社会（东西方文化互补与融合、互相推动，使人类逐步走向和谐世界发展），不知道会做何感想?

The Perfect Gift from China

Andrew Turner

For travellers to China, there is no shortage of souvenir choices to take home to family and friends. Perhaps one of the more interesting options is green tea grown with panda dropping fertilizer. It has become the world's most expensive tea but what could be more Chinese than pandas and tea?

来自中国的完美礼物

对来到中国的游客来说，为家人和朋友挑选纪念品带回家是不乏选择的。其中一个比较有意思的选择是用熊猫的排泄物制成的肥料培养出的绿茶。这种茶变成了世界上最贵的茶。但是还有什么比熊猫和茶更能代表中国的呢?

Chinese Steamed Buns

Heather Pfeiffer

My husband is from the north of China and one of his favourite things to eat is "baozi", or as we say in English "steamed buns". If abroad you should probably say "Chinese steamed buns" as the name is very general. His personal favourite is mutton or lamb, but some other good varieties are vegetable, black sesame seed, red bean, meatball and my personal favourite is spicy tofu. What type of filling do you enjoy?

中国包子

我的老公来自中国北方，他最爱吃的食物之一是包子，英语里叫作“steamed buns”，一种蒸出来的面食。尽管在国外，你或许会把“Chinese steamed buns”作为一个大致的统称。老公个人最爱吃的是羊肉或者羊羔肉馅儿的包子，另外他还喜欢吃蔬菜、黑芝麻、红豆、肉丸馅儿的。而我自己最爱的馅儿是麻辣豆腐。你喜欢什么馅儿的包子呢?

Asian Pears As Medicine

Heather Pfeiffer

I was sick again. My husband came home with some pears which he called Chinese medicine. Can you guess what I was sick with? I thought it was so strange that my husband was boiling pears with goji berries and what he called "ice sugar". This made me curious and after some research, here is what I found: Asian pears are good with honey in order to soothe the throat and reduce coughing. In English, "ice sugar" is known as rock sugar or rock candy. This sugar and goji berries (otherwise known as wolfberries) are used in many Chinese medicinal foods due to their general health benefits.

鸭梨是药吗?

我又生病了。我老公回家的时候，带回一种被他称作中药的鸭梨。你猜，令我感到最奇怪的是什么？我觉得奇怪的是，我老公在煮鸭梨的时候，还同时放入枸杞和被他称作冰糖的东西。这引起了我的好奇。经过一番搜寻之后，我发现：原来鸭梨和蜂蜜一起食用能利咽并且缓解咳嗽症状。在英语里，“ice sugar（冰糖）”亦被叫作“rock sugar”或者“rock candy”。这种糖和枸杞（亦作“wolfberries”）因其对身体的益处，常用在许多中药药膳里面。

Ginger and Red Sugar Water (a.k.a. Ginger and Brown Sugar Soup)

Heather Pfeiffer

It's another rainy day in Shanghai and my concerned, Chinese mother-in-law is bound to have already prepared some ginger and brown sugar soup for when I arrive home. In Chinese, this sugar is called "red sugar" but in English, we call it brown sugar. I'm told it will help me to sweat and decrease my chances of getting a cold. I'm not exactly 100% sold on the idea that it will stop a cold, but it can't hurt and the taste isn't half bad either.

红糖姜汤（也叫作：生姜黄糖汤）

又是一个上海的下雨天，我考虑周到的中国婆婆一定已经准备好了由姜和红糖熬成的汤等我回家。在中文里，这些糖被称作“红糖”，但是英语里，我们叫作“棕色的糖”。我得知它可以帮助身体发汗，并且能降低患感冒的概率。我并不百分百认同这种红糖姜汤能够预防感冒的说法，但是它对身体毕竟没有坏处，并且尝起来味道也还不错。

Tea Leaves or Tea Bags?

Rand Herz

Most places where people buy tea in the West you'll find the leaves sold in little bags, which you can steep in water in order to make tea. How different it is in the East! Here, people put the leaves directly in water. Sometimes it's difficult to drink, because you end up getting leaves in your mouth. Thoughtfully, some entrepreneurs have developed tea cups with screens to hold the leaves back. Personally, I prefer loose leaf tea. The tea bag is a little artificial and synthetic. Plus, drinking loose leaf tea, we can draw more infusions from the tea and get more from less! Very economic.

茶叶还是茶包?

在西方大多数地方，你会发现茶叶被装在小袋里出售。你可以把装有茶叶的茶包浸泡在水中，泡出茶汤。然而在东方，情况却大不相同！在这里，人们直接把茶叶放在水里。有时，这样喝起来不方便，因为你会把茶叶喝到嘴里。因此，一些考虑周到的企业，研发出带有茶叶过滤装置的茶杯，将茶叶阻隔在杯子里。个人而言，我更喜欢散装的茶叶。一来，茶包是人工合成的。二来，喝散装茶叶泡的茶，我们能从茶叶中浸泡出更多的茶汤，由少渐多，非常经济实惠！

Pumpkin or Squash

Heather Pfeiffer

Some things don't translate well in another language. Let me tell you about pumpkins and squashes. I love them! I particularly love butternut squash (makes a great soup!), but also spaghetti squash is pretty good (baked). In China, during this fall season, acorn squash is sold for pretty cheap. About two acorn squashes amount to one US dollar! Pumpkins have high sales in many western countries around this time because of Halloween. In Chinese, squash and pumpkin have the same name; this is because pumpkins are a type of squash, but in English, we have many names for all types of squashes! Mmmmm... this is making me hungry.

南瓜是pumpkin还是squash

有些事或物放在其他语言里翻译得并不好。让我和你聊聊“pumpkins”和“squashes”。我喜欢它们!

我尤其喜欢烤南瓜汤（butternut squash）（棒极了的一种汤！），但是（烤的）西葫芦汤也很好。在中国，在这样的秋天，青色南瓜卖得很便宜：两个小青南瓜加起来才一美元！现在这个时节，因为万圣节的关系，南瓜在许多西方国家变得非常畅销。在中文里，“squash”和“pumpkin”翻译的名字相同，都叫“南瓜”；这是因为南瓜（pumpkin）是南瓜属蔬菜（squash）中的一种。但是在英语里，南瓜属蔬菜中的每一种都有其特定的名字！嗯……讲到这儿，我感觉饿了。

Halloween Specialty Recipes

万圣节的食谱不再单调！下面就介绍一些有趣的万圣节创意食谱。

1. Frozen Banana Ghosts

Bananas taste spookily like creamy ice-cream when frozen in ghostly robes of white chocolate - quick and easy.

冰冻香蕉鬼

做成可爱幽灵形状的香蕉尝起来就像奶油冰激凌。这道菜的做法简便快捷，只要在香蕉外面抹上白巧克力，做成幽灵的样子，然后放在冰箱里冷冻一段时间，就可以啦！

2.Chocolate Bat Biscuits

Let a friendly bat perch on your glass of milk or cuppa this Halloween with these spooky biscuits - add vanilla butter cream for bourbons.

巧克力蝙蝠饼干

在这个万圣节，让可爱的小蝙蝠栖息在你的牛奶或者茶的杯沿。如果是搭配波本威士忌的话，可以再加上香草奶油。

3.Scary Halloween Jelly

Trick or treat time! This kids' party dessert may look gruesome, but the eyeballs and fingers are all sweet and fruity bites.

吓人的万圣节果子冻

“不招待就捣蛋”的时间到啦！这道为孩子们准备的节日甜点看上去可能有点吓人，但是那些眼球和手指其实都是糖果与水果制成的。

4.Orange Pumpkin Face Cookies

Great fun biscuits for trick-or-treaters - make a day or two ahead, then fill in before your spooky guests arrive.

橘子南瓜脸饼干

这是一款专门为“不招待就捣蛋”的孩子们准备的有趣饼干。在万圣节前一到两天准备好饼干，然后在你那些恐怖淘气的万圣节客人到来之前给它们加上馅儿、画上脸就可以啦！

5. Eyeball Pasta

Get everyone in the Halloween mood with this gory but tasty pasta dish.

眼球意大利面

让每个沉浸在万圣节气氛中的人，都能享受到恐怖又美味的意大利面大餐。

Longjing Tea

Andrew Turner

China is the birthplace of tea, and of the hundreds of tea varieties available perhaps Hangzhou West Lake Longjing tea is the most loved. It possesses the four qualities of a fine tea: attractive leaf shape, delicate fragrance, clear colour and fresh taste. Longjing tea is a true symbol of Chinese culture. How often do you drink it?

龙 井

中国是茶的发源地。而在成百上千的品种中，杭州西湖的龙井茶也许是最受人们喜爱的。它具备好茶的四大特质：诱人的茶叶形态，味道清香，色泽清爽，口感清新。龙井茶不愧是中国文化的真正象征。你多久品一次杭州西湖龙井茶?

Chinese Parks

Cher Reynolds

In the morning a small migration of Chinese people make their way to their local park. At 6am, you can join Chinese elders in the sport of Tai Chi. The later it gets the more colorful the park becomes. Now it's time for badminton or Chinese checkers under the trees. At noon, young couples and families take in the fresh air and maybe go fishing in the pond. The sky is dotted with kites and traditional songs are sung. Late afternoon, people head home to share dinner with their loved ones. Wonderful, magical Chinese parks bring people together from all generations.

中国式公园

早上，一群中国人朝公园走去。清晨6点，你可以跟着老年人练习打太极。时间越晚，公园里面进行的活动就越来越多姿多彩。清晨过后，是打羽毛球或者在树下下中国跳棋的时间。到了中午，年轻的夫妇和他们的家人来公园呼吸新鲜空气，或许还会在池边钓鱼。风筝伴着中国传统歌曲飞扬在公园上空。傍晚，人们都各自回家跟所爱的人共进晚餐。真的太美妙了！神奇的公园把每一代人都聚集在了一起。

Who Wears the Pants?

Allen Mak

While the general consensus in China is that men should still be the head of the household and make the important decisions, some women are starting to take a leadership role in the family. In some families, a woman is a mother, wife and breadwinner, sometimes taking care of the finances and the household duties. In Shanghai, it's said that Shanghainese men take care of the household, while their wives go out to earn money. So my question to you is, "Who wears the pants in your family?"

谁是一家之主?

尽管中国舆论普遍认为，男人应该是一家之主并且做重大决定的同时，一些女性已经开始在家中扮演领导的角色。在一些家庭中，女性同时承担了母亲、妻子以及养家糊口的角色，有时还要负责财务和家务。据说，在上海，妻子出去挣钱，男人则负责料理家务。因此，我的问题是，“在你家里，谁是一家之主？”

Do You Know Kung Fu?

Allen Mak

I was walking down the street of NYC and I saw some Chinese tourists being asked, "Hey buddy, do you know kung fu?" Many foreigners think that everyone in China knows kung fu or has learned it since primary school. But the truth is that only a small minority of people in China ever study kung fu. So beware of stereotypes, and also please don't believe that all black people can play basketball.

你了解功夫吗?

我走在纽约市的街道上，看到一些中国籍的游客正在被询问“嘿，朋友，你懂功夫吗？”许多外国人认为在中国人人都会功夫或是从小学起就开始学习功夫。但是事实是，仅有极小一部分的中国人曾学习过功夫。因此我们需要注意这样的思维定式，同样也别误认为所有的黑人朋友都会打篮球。

Animal Styles in Kung Fu

Kung fu is famous for its many animal styles, from frog to tiger and from **crane**（鹤） to snake, each with its own unique characterisics. The animal styles of kung fu are considered to be the "mother styles" of all Asian **martial arts**（武术）, based on the natural movements and fighting techniques of the tiger, the eagle, the crane, etc.

Do you know any other animal styles in kung fu?

Bittersweet

Andrew Turner

The bitter melon (ku gua) has been described as an ugly cucumber. However, despite its appearance, in Chinese medical tradition the bitter melon is valued for its medicinal properties, particularly that of lowering blood sugar levels. Apart from this, it is quite delicious when gently sautéed in black bean sauce!

苦中甜

“The bitter melon”（苦瓜）一直以来被描述成一种形状丑陋的类似黄瓜的蔬菜。但是，撇开它的外表，传统中医认为，苦瓜具有非常高的药用价值，尤其是在降血糖方面。另外，伴着豆豉清炒的苦瓜也很美味。

Chinatown

Tessa Xioutas

Did you know that Chinatown in San Francisco, California is the largest Asian community outside of China? "Chinatown" is an area in a country that's high in Chinese population. Here, you can enjoy the Chinese culture by shopping, eating and going to events. You can find a Chinatown in most large, western cities.

中国城（唐人街）

你知道位于加利福尼亚州旧金山的中国城吗？它是在中国之外，最大的一个亚洲人聚集区。中国城是一个国家里中国人居多的一块区域。在这里，你可以购物、吃饭以及参加一些活动，从中感受到中国文化的氛围。在西方几乎所有的大城市里，你都可以找到中国城。

Family VS. Career

Allen Mak

Do you spend more time on your career or with your family? I personally spend more time on my career. Not that I have much choice since my family is in the USA. Companies and businesses are becoming more globalized, so they will require us to do more business trips or even move abroad to work. Would you move abroad to work if your company asked you

to? It is a difficult choice to make. I have a friend who told me that he would never leave his wife or children for his career. Obviously, his values are with his family. So which do you value more?

家庭VS.工作

你花在工作上的时间多呢，还是花在家庭上的时间多呢？我个人花较多的时间在工作上。那是因为我的家人住在美国的缘故，所以我并没有太多其他的选择。当前，企业和生意都日趋全球化，这就需要我们出更多的差，甚至被派遣到海外工作。如果公司有要求，你愿意到海外工作吗？这是个很难的选择。我有一个朋友，他告诉我他绝对不会因为工作离开他的妻子或孩子。显然，他更重视家庭。那么对你而言，事业与家庭，哪个更为重要呢？

The Perseverance of Small Businesses

Allen Mak

In America, about 80% of small businesses fail within the first year. Many small businesses fail because the business owners have unrealistic expectations. They expect to make money within the first year and get rich within the second year. But in reality it isn't that easy, so they give up. If you are an entrepreneur, remember to have realistic expectations and most important to persevere.

微小企业坚持的重要性

在美国，80%的小企业在第一年内就宣告失败。许多小企业失败的原因是它们的老板都抱有不切实际的期望。他们期望在第一年就盈利，第二年就变得富有。但是在现实中，这样的期望并不容易实现，他们也就此放弃。如果你是一个企业家，切记要怀抱合乎现实的期望，以及最重要的是要坚持下去。

Chinese Women VS. Western Women

Allen Mak

I've heard many exaggerations about the differences between Chinese women and western women. Chinese women are more feminine, while western women are more independent. Chinese women are more docile, western women are more aggressive. The truth is that the different environments that Chinese and western women live in tend to shape them a certain way. But let's not exaggerate this. There are soft-spoken American women who prefer to be a stay home mom, and there are Chinese "superwomen" who dominate their fields. To stereotype women based only on their country of origin can be misleading.

中国女性VS.西方女性

我听说过许多关于中西方女性差异的夸张说法。中国女性更有女人味，而西方女性则更独立；中国女性更温柔，西方女性更强势。事实上，中西方女性所处不同的生活环境，塑造了她们不同的性格特点。但是我们不要夸大这些不同。有轻声细语、喜欢待在家做个母亲的美国女性，也有中国的“女超人”主导着她们所在的领域。仅凭女性的国籍来判断她们的特点往往具有误导性。

The Perfect Handshake Story

Lindsey Bard

Americans think a good handshake is very important. Offering only your fingers shows that you dislike the person because you don't want to touch them, while squeezing too hard means you want to intimidate them. A good handshake should squeeze just hard enough to test the ripeness of a peach.

什么是完美的握手

美国人认为一个恰到好处的握手非常重要。仅仅用手指握手表示你不喜欢这个人，因为你都不愿意碰触他们。而握手握得太紧表示你想威慑他们。一个完美的握手应该恰到好处，就好比你在挑选桃子时，看哪只更熟的时候而使的劲道。

在美国，恰到好处的握手是完美的礼仪呈现。但是，对于身体接触，不同文化有不同文化的理解。比如，尼泊尔人、斯里兰卡人和有些印第安人以及爱斯基摩人用点头表示“不”；阿拉伯人认为交谈的时候站得近些表示友好，而英国人则认为两个人之间保持一定的距离才是礼貌的。再说在美国，对于不同的交情，彼此之间选用的距离也是有讲究的。如果交谈双方关系亲密，比如是情侣，那么身体的距离从直接接触到相距约45厘米之间。朋友、熟人或亲戚之间个人交谈一般以相距45～80厘米为宜。而在进行一般社交活动时，交谈双方相距1.3～3米；在工作或办事时或者在大型的社交聚会上，交谈者一般保持1.3～2米的距离。

Chinese Marriage and In-laws

Allen Mak

Most western marriages are between two persons, while Chinese marriages are between a couple and their families. This means less conflict between a couple and their families in western marriages. I personally believe that everyone needs their personal space, and it's very difficult to have this when you're living with two persons who are not your parents and from a previous generation. How can you expect them not to favor their own child? How can you expect them to have the same lifestyle habits as you do? Perhaps living close and visiting often is a better choice than living together in close quarters.

中式婚姻和姻亲

大部分的西方婚姻是两个人之间的事情。然而，中国式婚姻却是夫妻和双方家庭的事情。西式婚姻意味着，夫妻与他们各自原生家庭之间的冲突较少。我认为，每个人都需要自己的空间，但跟非自己亲生父母的两位长辈同住时，就很难拥有自己的空间了。你怎么能期望他们不偏心自己的孩子呢？你怎么能期望他们跟你有相同的生活习惯呢？和与公婆或岳父岳母住在一起相比，也许住在他们附近并且经常走动看望会是更好的选择。

Hot or Cold

Allen Mak

I think most Chinese people must think I'm some sort of alien. I only drink cold water, and I eat ice-cream in the winter. I never wear "qiu ku" because I find it really uncomfortable. I'd rather freeze a bit. Many Chinese people have told me that drinking cold beverages is unhealthy for the body, and that I will catch a cold if I don't wear enough clothing. As an American that rejects hot water and hates itchy long underwear, I wish that my Chinese colleagues and friends would stop asking me if I'm cold!

热的还是冰的?

我想，大部分中国人会认为我是外星人。我只喝冰水，还在冬天吃冰淇淋。我从不穿“秋裤”，因为我觉得很不舒服，宁愿冻着。许多中国友人告诉我，喝冰水是不健康的；如果不穿够衣服我会感冒。作为一个美国人，我拒绝热水，讨厌又长又痒的秋裤。我希望中国的同事和朋友不要再问我冷不冷啦！

Philanthropy

Rand Herz

Many say that in order to receive, you have to give, first. In fact, the so-called "Golden Rule", which has been written in every major civilization's history, is "Give and you shall receive".

This is the basis of the practice of philanthropy: giving to others. Maybe you won't get anything material back, but the feeling of making a positive impact on others' lives is one of the most rewarding.

See if you can find a charity or cause to donate to in your own city. You may have the initiative, even, to begin your own non-profit organization. Many people are in need. Some of us have more than others. Let's help each other build a wealthier civilization.

善 行

许多人都说要想得到就得先付出。实际上，这个所谓的“黄金法则”几乎被写入每一段重要的文明史中，那就是“付出就会有回报”。

这是一个做善事的基础：给予他人。可能你并不能得到任何物质的回报，但是给别人的生活带来正面影响的感觉，就是最好的回报。

看看你是否能在当地找到可捐赠的慈善机构。你也可以主动地，甚至自己开始创办一个非营利的机构。许多人都需要帮助。而我们中的一些比其他人拥有更多。让我们互相帮助，共建一个更富足的文明社会。

My Visit to Beijing

Monroe Mann

Last month, I visited Beijing for the first time. I made the mistake of visiting this great city during National Day. Big mistake: the crowds of people were insurmountable. Trying to walk around Tian'anmen Square was a nightmare. I have to go back there again some day, when it is NOT a public holiday!

我的北京之旅

上个月，我第一次去北京。选择在国庆节期间参观这座大城市是一个错误。最大的问题是：我很难应对拥挤的人群。在这个时候逛天安门广场是一场噩梦。所以我打算重游北京，当然是在非国定节假日的时候。

Riding My Bike

Monroe Mann

I love riding my bike in Shanghai for a number of reasons. First, the landscape is flat. There are not many hills. Second, there are many bike lanes throughout the city. Finally, it is very easy to park my bicycle because there are designated parking areas early everywhere!

骑自行车

我喜欢在上海骑自行车有许多的原因。第一，上海地势平坦，没有许多的山地。第二，它的自行车道多且覆盖整个城市。最后，停车方便，因为指定的停车区域随处可见！

Chapter 3 Always Learning 求知·守拙

"Once you stop learning, you start dying." said Albert Einstein. These are some thoughts about learning and developing from our authors. We hope that they will inspire you to continue learning!

阿尔伯特·爱因斯坦曾说过："当你停止学习之时，便是迈向死亡的开始。"我们希望接下来由我们外教老师创作的文章可以在某种程度上激励你们继续在求知的道路上不断前行。

Ways the Digital Age Is Changing the Face of Education

Allen Mak

The digital age has started to extend its reach into education. Now 100% of American universities are using social media to connect with their students, and top schools are developing their e-learning programs to save money and time. Most schools are predicted to have a hybrid learning environment in the near future, combining online and offline education. Some have even predicted that there will be fewer than 10 universities in 50 years, as online education will have rendered brick-and-mortar schools obsolete. Online courses will also make

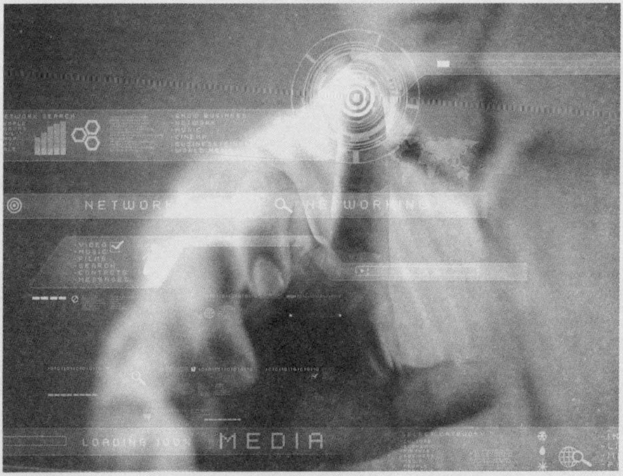

education accessible to people of all walks of life, encouraging passion-based learning and continuing education. Do you think offline education will be obsolete in the future?

数码时代正在改变教育的面貌

教育领域也迎来了数字时代。现在几乎所有的美国大学都在使用社会化媒体与学生互动交流。一些顶尖的学校正在大力发展在线教育课程，以此节省经济与时间成本。预计大部分的学校在不久的将来，都能拥有混合型的学习环境以及线上和线下相结合的教育方式。有人甚至预测，未来50年大学的数量不会超过10所！因为在线教育将打破校舍的水泥围墙，使各行各业的人都能接受教育，并鼓励充满激情的、不断的学习。你认为线下教育将来真的会被淘汰吗?

MOOCs: Massive Online Open Courses

Allen Mak

MOOCs are gaining in popularity around the world. They provide free online courses to the masses in which anyone can study various kinds of subjects. This appeals to many learners who wish to pursue adult education, also known as continuing education. Currently they are still in the experimental period and investors are trying to monetize MOOCs. If you get a chance, you should check out a MOOC because they won't be free forever!

大型开放式网络课程

大型开放式网络课程越来越受到全世界的欢迎。MOOC面向大众提供免费的线上课程，任何人都能学习各个科目的课程。这个平台满足了众多希望继续获取成人教育的学习者的需求，所以又叫作继续教育。目前，大型开放式课程还处在试运行阶段，投资者试图货币化这种大型开放式的网络课程。如果有机会，你应该看看网上的开放式课程，显然它们不会永远免费。

耶鲁大学提供网络公开课（**Open Yale Courses**）是耶鲁大学在2007年12月启动的一个项目。此项目是耶鲁大学在它的网站上（**Yale Online website**）分享其本科课堂的全程录像。此项目目前包括42门在耶鲁大学本科教授的课程。一开始，这个项目是由惠利基金（**William and Flora Hewlett Foundation**）资助的，它也资助其他大学的一些公开课项目。2014年8月，耶鲁大学的开放课程登陆北欧在线教育编辑平台（**Eliademy**）。感兴趣的朋友们还在等什么呢？轻击鼠标，尽情享受耶鲁大学的学霸待遇吧！

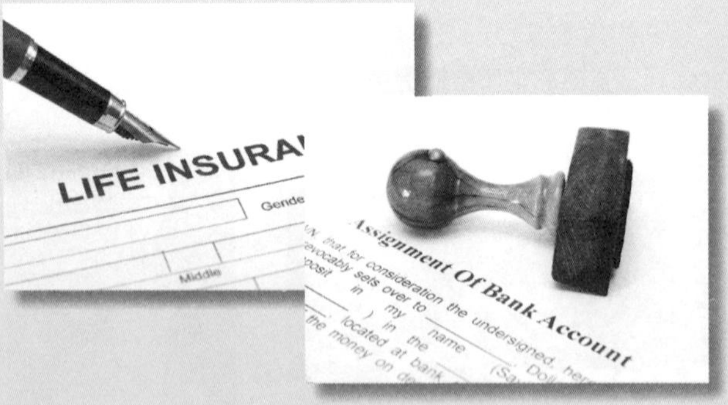

Digital Education in the United States

Allen Mak

In the US, many states and districts have launched online public schools that allow children at all ages to attend school from the comfort of their own homes. Currently, there are an estimated 250,000 students enrolled in online schools across the United States, as well as two million who have taken at least one course online. Advocates of online education believe that this will save money and provide a more tailored and personalized education for students. Teachers are still involved with students' education, either by answering questions through phone, text, or email. Will digital education take over the future?

美国数字化教育

在美国，许多州和地区开办了网上公立学校，这些学校允许任何年龄的儿童在舒适的家中学习。目前，全美估计有250 000名学生注册了在线学校，同时还有两百万的学生在线学习了至少一门课程。网络教育的倡导者相信，这将为美国各州节省开支并且为学生提供更加量体裁衣的个性化教育课程。当然，老师们还是会参与到学生的学习中去，可以通过电话、短信或是电子邮件的方式回答问题。数字化的教育在将来会取代传统教育模式吗？

The Benefits of E-learning for Language Courses

Allen Mak

E-learning is a combination of both traditional learning environments and modern technological advances that differ from instructor-focused courses and self-study. Online education provides the student with an opportunity to listen to native speakers (preventing embarrassing pronunciation or grammatical errors); work with classmates from all over the world (instead of a few classmates in a traditional classroom); and repeat and study coursework at their own pace. More importantly, online courses can be done at your convenience, whether it is 30 minutes on your lunch break or after dinner when you have some free time, unlike traditional classes that require you to be at a fixed place at a fixed time. Flexible learning will be the future.

E-learning在线语言课程的益处

E-learning是传统教学环境和现代先进技术结合的一种学习方式，它与以教员为中心的授课方式或者自学都有所不同。在线学习为学生提供了倾听母语者授课的机会（避免了尴尬的发音或者语法错误）；与来自世界各地的同学们一起上课（而非传统课堂里那数量有限的学习同伴）；并且，复习、做作业都按自己的节奏进行。更重要的是，在线学习可以在你闲暇的时候，不管是30分钟的午餐时间或是饭后的一些自由时间，你都可以自由地学习，而非传统的需要你在特定的时间、地点学习的模式。灵活的学习方式将会成为未来教育的发展方向。

Available Space – This Is Not About Learning

Andrew Turner

In 1998, the first 32-megabyte MP3 player could hold from 10 to 20 songs.

In 2005, a 60-gigabyte MP3 player could hold about 13,000 songs.

In 2013, a 1-terabyte MP3 player can hold more than 240,000 songs. That's over one year's continuous listening time!

Big, bigger and bigger still - all within fifteen years!

What will the next step be? In 2020, will we consider 1-terabyte to be too small?

存储空间

1998年，第一台32兆的MP3播放器可以存储10～20首的歌曲。

2005年，60千兆字节的MP3播放器可以存储13 000首歌曲。

2013年，1太字节的MP3可以存储超过240 000首歌曲。那相当于花上超过一年的时间连续不间断地听，才能听完这些歌曲。

大的、更大的，比更大还要大的存储空间（的诞生）——这些在短短十五年间都实现了！

那么，再接下来会发生什么呢？到了2020年，我们是否会觉得太字节只是很小的空间呢？

Is It the End for Paperback Books?

Allen Mak

Have you ridden the subway to work recently? Last week, I was riding the subway to work and I saw an interesting change, which I should have noticed long ago. Subway commuters weren't reading paperback books. It seemed everyone had an e-book reader. So the question is, "Will paperback books be replaced soon?"

Many businesses would rather sell e-books now to cut down on the cost. The cost of importing, warehousing, and shipping books is certainly a burden for businesses. What do you think? Is it time for paperbacks disappear? Or do you prefer keeping books on your bookshelf and stacked in the basement?

平装书的时代终结了吗?

你最近有乘坐地铁上班吗？上个礼拜，我乘地铁上班，发现了一个我本该很早就注意到的有趣的变化。地铁里的乘客没有在阅读平装书，而是看上去每个人都在使用电子阅读器进行阅读。所以我的问题是，“平装书将很快被取代了吗？”

现在，许多商家更愿意出售电子书来降低成本。进口、仓库存储以及交通运输所产生的成本对商家来说无疑都是一个负担。你怎么认为呢？平装书是时候该消失了吗？还是你依旧喜欢在你的书架上摆放平装书，看完后再把它们存放到地下室去呢？

What is e-book？

An electronic book (e-book) is a book-length publication in **digital form**（电子形式），**consisting of**（包括）text, images, or both, and you should read it on computers or other **electronic devices**（电子设备）. Apparently, it is not only **"an electronic version of a printed book"**（已出版书的电子版）,as many e-books exist without any **printed version**（印刷版本）. **Commercially produced and sold**（商业化生产和出售的）e-books are usually intended to be read on **dedicated e-book readers**（专用的电子书阅读器）.

Blended Learning VS. Traditional Learning Method

Allen Mak

Question: "What is it that is always changing?" Answer: "It is change itself!" Teaching and learning methods have also been changing throughout history.

Traditional learning methods focus on knowledge flowing downwards from teacher to student, master to pupil, or trainer to trainee.

Blended learning is about learning from multiple sources in your surroundings. It means that you can learn from your teacher, your peers, your computer, and etc. It is also about constantly learning and applying what you have learned in your surroundings.

Which style of learning do you prefer? It is a good question, and only you have the answer!

混合学习法VS.传统学习法

什么是在一直变化着的？答案是，变化本身。教与学的方法，一直随着历史的发展发生着变化。

传统的学习法专注于知识自上而下的传授：老师教学生，导师带弟子，培训师训练受训的人。

混合学习法是指利用你身边的各种资源去学习。也就是说，你可以跟你的老师学习，也可以和你的同伴学习，还可以通过使用电脑进行学习，等等。它是一种不间断的、持续性的学习，然后把你学到的再运用到你所处的环境中。

你喜欢哪种学习方式呢？这是个好问题，只有你知道问题的答案。

Language Exposure

Rand Herz

Many people try to learn languages. Many people do not succeed. These people do not realize one critical aspect of learning languages. When you learn a language, you must use it.

If you read about sailing in a classroom and practice in a classroom, but then never set foot on a boat; will you ever become a competent sailor? No.

Likewise for language. In order to master it, you must use it. Find some English-speaking friends. Read English magazines. Listen to English songs, TV shows and radio stations. Live in English. Only then will you become proficient.

使用语言

许多人都会尝试学习语言。但他们中的很多都没能成功。这些人没意识到：学习语言很重要的一点就是当一个人在学语言时，你必须使用这门语言。

这就好比你在课堂上学习有关航海的知识并且在课堂上练习航海的不同技巧，但是你从没上过船，那你有可能变成出色的水手吗？答案显然是，绝对不可能。

学习语言也是如此。要完全掌握一门语言，你必须去运用这门语言。找一些说英语的朋友、读英文杂志、听英文歌、看英文节目以及听英文广播。生活在英语当中，只有这样你才能精通英语。

怎样在繁忙的日常生活中尽量多地使用英语?

Eric Friedman

致力于打造“有效沟通”，即教会学生如何在真正专业的商务环境中去使用英语的华尔街英语给想在繁忙的日常生活中营造出学习英语氛围的朋友们两点友情建议：

首先，遵循学习的自然规律——从听开始。听一段场景，然后进行重复，重复关键的词语和句型，练习和纠正发音，理解词语的意思，然后通过每周两到三次的练习去强化、巩固。如果你能够置身于一个能够和以英语为母语的人交流对话的环境中那是最理想不过的事情，如果缺乏这样的环境，那不妨从观看一部英语原版影片入手。

另外一个建议是：不要胆怯，请放手让自己练习开口说英语，去积极地使用这门语言。沟通的关键在于对于语言的掌握和运用。前提是你要做好足够的心理建设之后，才能让自己非常舒服和自如地用英语对话，勇于练习使用不同的英语表达方式，只有克服了这样的障碍，你才能够获得一段成功的学习体验。

Everyday Listening

Rand Herz

Listening may be one of the easiest language skills, next to reading, writing and speaking. Listening is utterly passive. You only have to use your ears. You can do it with your eyes closed. You can do it anywhere!

It's easy to find English materials online to listen to; especially at Apple's iTunes store. There are plenty of free podcasts that you can download as an MP3 file and put onto your computer or MP3 player.

Check some out and try to get in 15 to 20 minutes of listening practice, or more, a day! Everyday practice is essential to improvement.

天天听力

听力可能是最简单的语言技巧之一，比阅读、写作以及口语都要容易。听力完全是接受信息的行为，只需要使用自己的耳朵。你可以闭上自己的眼睛做听力练习，可以在任何一个地方做听力练习！

在网上找听力材料是很容易的，尤其在苹果的iTunes商店。那里有许多免费的音频，可以下载成MP3格式，存到你的电脑上或者是放进MP3播放器里。

去找一些音频，然后每天做15到20分钟或更长时间的听力练习！坚持每天的听力练习对英语的进步是很重要的。

How to Remember New Words: Associations

Heather Pfeiffer

Trying to learn new words? Here is a helpful tip-always keep in mind that remembering new words has to do with associations. For example, you join an English corner about bugs. You don't know what "bug" means, but the teacher shows many pictures of worms, mosquitoes, cockroaches, etc. These pictures will help

you remember and are a kind of association. Then you remember last night you saw a cockroach on the floor - yikes! If you can connect a new word to a picture and then a memory, you will remember it better.

如何记住新单词：学会联想

尝试学习新的单词？在这里分享一个有用的贴士：时时记着在记忆新词的过程中要学会联想。例如，你参加以虫为主题的英语角。你不知道“bug（虫子）”的英文意思，但是你的老师展示了好多蠕虫、蚊、蟑螂的图片，等等。这些图片可以帮你记住“bug”的意思，而这就是一种很好的联想。那么你就会记得昨晚看见“cockroach（蟑螂）”在地板上。对，就是这样！ 如果你能学会运用画面来进行联想，然后记忆，你就可以更好地牢记这个单词。

Vocabulary Building

Rand Herz

For students, one of the scariest tasks is learning new words. Many students are overwhelmed by building a vocabulary.

Here are some tips to help you:

(1)Learn words in groups. For example, study types of clothing and clothes-related words all in one week.

(2)Build lists and carry them with you; you can review them several times daily. Use the words in conversation.

(3)Learn all forms of a word. For example, when you learn "politics", you can learn "politician" (n.), "political" (adj.) and "politically" (adv.).

词汇拓展

对于初学者，一个最令人畏惧并且困难的任务就是学习新的单词。许多学生都被拓展词汇量所打倒。

要克服这个挑战，有以下建议：

(1)分组学词。例如，用一周时间专门学习与衣服类型以及与衣服相关的英文词汇。

(2)制作单词表并且随身携带；你可以每天复习几次，并将单词用到你和他人的对话当中。

(3)学习某个单词的不同形式。例如，当你学习单词“politics（政治）”时，你可以同时学习它的几种不同形式，比如，“politician （政客）n.（名词）”以及“political（政治的）adj.（形容词）”“politically（政治地）adv.（副词）”。

Socratic Method of Learning

Heather Pfeiffer

Socrates was one of the most famous Greek philosophers. He is famous for saying, "I know that I know nothing". From this idea came what we call the Socratic method, a technique of learning by asking questions. Questions are an active way to study because it keeps the learner constantly engaged. If someone asks questions about what you learning, the amount of information you retain and understand greatly increases as opposed to being a passive listener or only self-studying. Find a teacher, colleague or friend to ask you questions about learning English.

苏格拉底学习法

苏格拉底是希腊著名的哲学家之一 。就如苏格拉底的名言："我知道我一无所知。"从这一观点出发，发展成为我们今天所说的苏格拉底教学法。它是一套提问的学习技巧。问答是一种积极的学习方法，因为它让学习者时刻保持专注。与被动听课的人或者自学者相比，如果某人问你有关学习的问题时，你能记住的信息量以及对信息的理解程度就会大大提升。找一个老师、同事或者朋友，让他们问问你关于英语学习的问题吧。

Helicopter Parents

Philip Simpson

It is the first day of school. All the mothers are standing at the gate crying as their babies walk into the building to start their journey as a student. This is a very uncomfortable experience for many parents, as their children take their first steps towards being independent. However, some parents really struggle to let go; they start to regularly call the school to try and find out more about what their children are up to. They may even start "helping" with their kids' homework (and by helping I mean doing it for them). For some parents they may even continue this behavior when their children are at university! We call them helicopter parents, because they are always hovering just above their children, keeping a close eye on them!

直升机式父母

开学的第一天，所有的妈妈哭着站在学校大门口，因为她们的宝贝走进了学校大楼，开始学生生涯了。对于许多父母来说这可不好过，因为他们的孩子向着独立迈出了第一步。然而，一些父母还是挣扎着不肯放手。他们开始定期打电话到学校，以便知道他们的孩子在做什么；他们甚至开始辅导孩子的作业（辅导是指帮他们的孩子写作业）。甚至一些父母，在他们小孩进入大学了还继续这么做。我们称他们为“直升机式父母”（helicopter parents），因为他们总是在孩子的头顶上空盘旋，密切地关注着他们的孩子们！

Parental Involvement in School Life and Policy

Allen Mak

Western parents have more control over the day to day operations of the schools that their children attend. In eastern schools, the Principals and teachers have almost total authority although recent changes in the laws, especially in South Korea, are beginning to change that culture. Changes to the school schedule, curriculum, even the lunches provided to students come under the inspection of parents and many times are voted on by panels representing the community the school serves. As a contrast, western schools will notify parents of changes, however, parents largely are powerless to affect change if they desire.

家长影响校园生活和政策

以前，西方的父母对孩子们每天的学校生活控制得更多；而在东方的学校，校长和老师几乎是拥有至高无上的权威。尽管，最近以韩国为代表的相关法律的变化正在改变这种文化：学校的时间表、课程甚至提供给学生的午餐的变化都在家长的监督之下，而这些改变多数都是由家长代表小组投票决定的。相比而言，西方学校更多的是会告诉学生的父母正在发生的变化，但是大部分的父母还是不具备足够的影响力去促成一些他们所期望的改变。

在这两篇文章中，我们讨论了与父母有关的话题。那么在现在社会中，到底怎样才算是理想的父母呢？是直升机父母爱的教育感人，还是所谓的“虎妈狼爸”的权威更能震慑住孩子们呢？下面就是Allen Mak所设想的理想父母模式。

I'm sure many of you have heard of these three interesting ways of parenting. It kind of reminds me of the different kinds of **martial arts stance**（武术招式） we have. Like tiger stance, snake stance, **crane**（鹤） stance, etc. It's really funny, but sad at the same time that we need to use such extreme parenting methods to bring up our children. There's no one style of parenting because all children are different. As parents we need to adapt our parenting style when needed. **Flexibility**（灵活性）and **adaptability**（适应性）is probably the most important method when it comes to parenting. So which animal is flexible and adaptable? The Snake! Next time I will write a book on Snake Dad!

Happiness

Mann Monroe

Many psychologists believe that happiness is partly based on your genes and partly based on your attitude. In other words, while in some way, your happiness levels are fixed, you ARE able to control your happiness to some extent, based on how you think about things.

幸 福

许多心理学家认为幸福感一部分由基因决定，一部分取决于你自身的态度。也就是说，从某种程度上来说，你的快乐程度是固定的，你能够控制自己的幸福感，这基于你如何看待事物。

Dreams

David Gilmour

I'm really interested in dreams. I think they can tell us a lot about what we are really thinking and how we really feel. There are some common dreams such as flying and falling. I often wake up suddenly because I feel like I am falling. I have a reoccurring dream of skating around and falling backwards. I asked my grandmother what it meant and she told me I needed to skate better!

梦

我对梦很感兴趣，我认为它可以告诉我们许多自己内心的真正想法以及真实感受。有一些常见的梦，比如（在空中）飞行以及（从高处）坠落。我常常因为在梦中坠落而突然惊醒。我会重复做一个梦：我在滑冰却一直落后于人。我问奶奶这个梦暗示了什么，她告诉我，这个梦是提醒我需要滑得更好！

梦的功能

人们对梦的研究一直不断。弗洛伊德曾在《梦的解析》中提到，梦表达的是人类遭受压抑的欲望。一些时候确实如此，但近年来的一些研究调查也显示，人们甚至可以利用梦来处理信息或者储存记忆。此外，人类在浅层睡眠和深层睡眠中都会做梦。其中，在浅度睡眠时的梦境里，人们会爆发更多的情感，因此梦境中的冲突增加并且显得戏剧化、不真实，同时有可能向噩梦发展。而熟睡状态时做的梦大多会涉及友好的社交互动，显得更和谐、逼真。据调查，受到压抑的人往往比生活得较轻松的人更容易受到噩梦的困扰。而前几年大热的影片《盗梦空间》也是基于《梦的解析》对梦境研究的精彩演绎。

Chapter 4 Healthy Body, Healthy Mind

运动·乐活

Ancient doctors in both the East and the West came up with the idea of the healthy mind in a healthy body, and how one will support the other. Read the following articles for ideas about health and happiness.

古时候，东方和西方的医生就已经得出了，只有健康的身体才能孕育出健康心灵的结论，可见体魄和心灵两者是互相支撑、不可分离的。下面的文章会和你分享更多关于健康与幸福的话题。

Jeremy Lin "The Underdog Story"

Allen Mak

Who is Jeremy Lin? I'm sure many of you know him. He is currently the most popular basketball star in the NBA. Go ahead and google him. You will see thousands of articles about him. But the question is "Why is he so popular?" I'll keep it short and simple. Lin represents me and you. He stands for the common people because he doesn't have Shaq's physique, Yao Ming's height, nor does he have Kobe's talent. But what he has is "heart". His perseverance, hard work, and heart tell us all that even common people can succeed. That's right! We can succeed too, if we persevere and never give up our dreams. So let us show the world our "heart of fire".

林书豪——黑马的故事

谁是林书豪？我相信很多人都知道他。他是当下NBA里最热门的球星。去网上搜索一下他，你将会看到成千上万关于他的文章。但问题是，他为什么这么受欢迎呢？简而言之，因为林书豪代表了你我。他代表了平凡的大众，因为他既没有“大鲨鱼”奥尼尔的体格，也没有姚明的身高以及科比的天赋。然而，他拥有一颗火热的心。他的坚持不懈、他的努力进取还有他的心，都告诉我们，即使是平凡人也可以获得成功。是的！只要我们坚持不懈，永不放弃我们的梦想，我们也可以成功。那么，让我们向世界秀出我们火热的心吧！

Plank

Allen Mak

A plank is a new type of exercise which is getting really popular in America. It is a strength exercise that involves maintaining a difficult position for extended periods of time. The plank helps build up your abs and your lower back which is very important for your overall body. So start doing some planks and to improve your overall health!

平板支撑

平板支撑是一种新型的运动，目前在美国变得越来越流行。 它是一种力量型运动，有时需要长时间维持一个高难度的姿势。平板支撑帮助你锻炼腹肌，以及对全身很重要的下背部的力量。那么现在就做一些平板支撑，开始改善你的健康状况吧！

Water Sports

Tessa Xioutas

Have you ever been snorkeling or scuba diving? These are both water sports. Snorkeling is when you have a mask and a tube. Scuba diving is when you have a mask and an air tank; this allows you to stay in the water longer and go deeper. Both are great ways to see all the wonderful fish in the sea!

与水相关的运动

你潜过水或者试过水肺潜水吗？它们都是水上运动。潜水时，你需要戴上口罩、插上水管。水肺潜水时，你要戴上口罩并且背上氧气瓶，这使你在水下待的时间更长，游得更深。两种方式都是观赏水下美丽壮观的鱼群的好方法哦！

Scuba Diving

Cher Reynolds

The ocean is full of wonders, slippery seaweed, frolicking fish, creeping crustaceans, diving dolphins and wallowing whales. We can study the life of the ocean by watching documentaries; however some people like to get much closer to the action. Have you ever tried scuba diving? Put on your wet suit, flippers, mask, oxygen tank and dive deep into the ocean. This activity allows us to breathe underwater with the help of an oxygen tank and swim like a fish using the flippers. Scuba diving is a great way to keep fit and have an adventure at the same time!

水肺潜水

海洋充满了神奇的生物：滑溜溜的水草，嬉戏的鱼类，缓慢蠕动的甲壳纲动物，跳水的海豚，还有欢乐打滚的鲸。我们可以通过看相关题材的纪录片了解海洋生物。然而，一些人喜欢通过行动来亲近海洋。你曾经试过水肺潜水吗？穿上你的紧身潜水衣，戴上脚蹼、面罩，背上氧气罐，然后潜入深海中。这样的活动，需要我们在氧气罐的帮助之下进行水下呼吸，然后像穿了脚蹼的鱼一样游来游去。潜水是一种保持身材的好方法且同时也是一种冒险！

Ten Reasons Why You Should Swim

Heather Pfeiffer

Do you know how to swim? Do you swim often? If you're answer was no to either of these questions, here's a few reasons why you should consider swimming more. Firstly, swimming works out ALL, yes all, of your major muscle groups, as well as improves natural flexibility for children. Next, it gives a full-body work out without the sprains, strains and bruises; swimming has less injuries than any other sport. Not to mention, swimming lowers stress levels and blood pressure. So enjoy the health benefits and paddle around your local pool!

应该游泳的理由

你会游泳吗？你经常游泳吗？如果你的回答都是“不”的话，你就应该考虑多游泳了。第一，游泳帮助锻炼全身，它之所以锻炼全身，在于它锻炼了身体的主要肌肉群，同时还能改善小孩子身体的柔韧性。其次， 在不拉伤、扭伤或是擦伤的情况下，游泳能使全身都得到充分的锻炼。相比其他运动，游泳引起的运动损伤是较少的。更不用说，游泳还有减缓压力和降低血压的作用。还不赶紧去你家附近的游泳馆，享受游泳给健康带来的益处！

The Power of Wristband

Andrew Turner

Many athletes around the world wear sports wristbands. Some are purely decorative but some are said to increase the wearer's focus, concentration, balance, strength, flexibility and natural energy. Some even claim to block harmful radiation and enhance healing. Are they a placebo, fashionable fad, scientific breakthrough or just good marketing?

手环的能量

世界各地有许多运动员都会佩戴运动手环。有些人纯粹是为了装饰，而有一些手环佩戴者，据说是为了集中精力，提高专注力、平衡感，增加力量、灵活性以及提升自然的能量。一些手环甚至号称具有阻挡辐射和治疗的功效。这些手环是一种心理安慰，还是代表了一种时尚流行，又或是科技上的突破，抑或仅仅是一种有效的产品营销手法呢?

Wearable Technology

Allen Mak

Imagine that you buy a pair of shoes which can measure how tired your legs are or a shirt which measures your blood sugar level. This is what we call wearable technology. The main purpose of the technology is to support human beings with real time data which we can use to make better decisions with. Would you like it if your shoes inform you that your legs are tired, and maybe it's time to rest?

可佩戴式科技

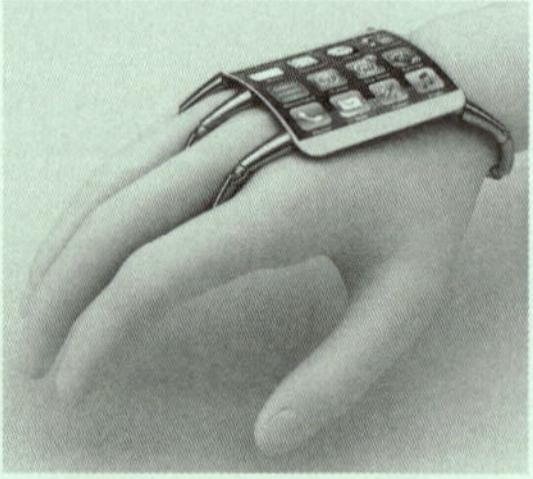

试想一下，你买了一双鞋，而这双鞋能够测量你的腿有多疲劳；或者，你买了一件衬衫，它能够测量你的血糖有多高。这就是我们所说的可佩戴式科技。可佩戴式科技的主要目的是以实时数据辅助人们做出更好的决定。如果你的鞋子能够告诉你，你的腿已经累了，是时候需要休息一下了，你会不会觉得这样的鞋子很棒?

可佩戴式科技现在越来越多地出现在我们的生活中。比如谷歌（**Google**）推出的谷歌眼镜（**Google Project Glass**），该款眼镜将运行Android智能操作系统，不仅能进行视频通话，还能进行拍照、上网等几乎所有手机所具有的功能。而Whistle公司则专门为宠物狗研发出了一种可佩戴式跟踪设备，可检测狗的活动和健康状况，让主人不再担心爱犬走失或者生病。印度开发了防强奸内衣（**The Anti-rape Lingerie**），该产品配备全球定位系统模块和GSM移动通信模块，能够在女性遭到性侵犯时通知其家人和警察，并向歹徒发射高压电流。随着科技的进步，我们的生活将变得更加便捷与安全。

Warm Up

Heather Pfeiffer

It's important to warm up before you begin exercise. This can include jogging for a few minutes, doing some stretches, jumping jacks, etc. To warm up means to exercise in preparation for something, such as a sport. Stretching, jogging and doing jumping jacks are good ways to prepare your body for vigorous physical activity. Finally, warm ups can also be preparations before other activities that can

be challenging, such as your voice before singing or your mind before taking a test. So what do you do to warm up?

热身运动

在开始锻炼之前做好充分的热身运动是很重要的。热身运动可以是几分钟的慢跑，或是做些拉伸、蹦跳运动，等等。“To warm up”是指为某事做准备练习，比如说运动。拉伸、慢跑，还有开合跳，都是为剧烈的体育运动做好准备活动的方法。此外，这个词组也可以指在开始进行其他富有挑战性的活动之前所做的准备工作。例如，你在唱歌之前要做开嗓练习，或者在考试之前会做思考练习。那么通常你会怎么热身呢?

Football Culture in the UK

Cher Reynolds

You may already know that in England football is a really big deal! Football is a huge part of British culture and most English people grow up playing it, watching it or both! England has many football teams that are famous worldwide; these teams also have many fans in China. Arsenal, Manchester United and Liverpool are three of the most renowned teams from England. Most English people will grow up following their home team; Sunday is match day, when you put on your football shirt and head on down to the football stadium to watch the match of the day with friends and family, or go to the local pub to watch the match on TV or even gather family together at your own home to cheer on the local team. Whichever you choose is guaranteed to be a whole lot of fun no matter if your team wins or loses.

英国的足球文化

你可能已经知道，在英格兰，足球真的是一件举足轻重的事！在英国文化里，足球扮演了一个很重要的角色；而且大部分英国人就是在踢足球、看足球或是两者兼有中成长起来的。英格兰有很多享誉世界的知名球队，在中国也有很多它们的球迷。阿森纳（Arsenal）、曼彻斯特联队（Manchester United）、利物浦（Liverpool）是英格兰三支最知名的球队。大部分的英格兰人都伴着他们家乡的主队成长。星期天是球赛日，穿上你的球衣并且前往足球场，一整天跟朋友或者家人待在一起看比赛；或者去当地的酒吧，观看电视转播赛事；更或是在自己家中，一家人聚在一起为本地足球队加油。无论你选择哪种方式，无论你支持的队是赢或输，你都能尽兴。

足球流氓

英国人对足球是狂热的。而英国的足球流氓事件也是世界皆知的。英文中，"football hooligan"的意思就是"足球流氓"。"Hooligan"一词最初是爱尔兰家族的一个姓氏。19世纪末，Patrick Hooligan是伦敦东部远近闻名的流氓恶少，因此后来他的姓氏"Hooligan"一词也就逐渐演变为"流氓"的意思。

足球流氓是世界性的，每个国家都有足球流氓，其中以英国的足球流氓最为著名。足球流氓一般具有以下特点：首先，近乎职业性地到足球赛事上寻衅滋事，一旦有大的赛事，他们就一定会到那里集结；再之，闹事第一，看球第二；三是，他们每次一闹，必要闹大、甚至会造成人员伤亡。英国的"足球流氓"臭名昭著，不仅英国警方把他们列入了监控名单，凡是举办国际性赛事的国家、地区的警方，对他们也都严阵以待，有的根本不允许他们入境。

Fair Weather Fans

Philip Simpson

Do you like to watch football? How about basketball? Whatever your sport may be, you will find the fair weather fan. This is an expression used to talk about somebody who only likes a team when they are doing well. Sometimes the fair weather fan will change which team to follow when his old team is not winning! In most western countries you don't choose which team you support, but follow the local team or the team your father supported instead. That's why my team is Sunderland, not Chelsea or Manchester United...it's in my blood!

伪球迷

你喜欢看足球比赛吗？那么篮球比赛呢？不管是什么样的运动，你都会找到伪球迷（“fair weather fan” 又叫晴天球迷）。这个短语指的是，只有在球队打得不错时，才喜欢该球队的那些人。有时，当原先喜欢的球队不再赢得比赛时，伪球迷就会改变他们拥护的球队。在大多数西方国家中，通常你不用选择自己支持的球队，而是拥护本地的球队或者你爸爸拥护的队。这也是为什么，我支持的队是桑德兰，而不是切尔西或者曼联等，这种支持是与生俱来的！

Unusual Sports

Heather Pfeiffer

A sport that you may not have heard of, cheese rolling, has been played in Gloucestershire, England for the last two hundred years. First, a cylindrical block of hard cheese is rolled down a hill; the idea is that competitors race to catch the cheese (though this is near impossible since the cheese may roll at a speed of approximately 60 plus miles per hour). The first person to reach the bottom of the hill wins. While this seems simple enough, the steepness of the hill usually causes mild to semi-severe injuries, such as broken bones and sprains. Therefore, a few ambulances are always present at this annual competition.

另类体育

滚奶酪大赛（cheese rolling），可谓一项鲜为人知的体育运动。在英格兰的格洛斯特郡，这个比赛已经有两百年历史了。首先，一个圆柱形的硬奶酪块从山上滚下来；选手（competitors）争抢滚下来的奶酪（尽管这几乎是不可能的，因为奶酪可能以每小时60多英里的速度滚动），第一个到达山脚的人赢得比赛。这项运动虽然看起来很简单，然而陡峭的山势常常会使选手受轻伤甚至较严重的伤，例如骨折或扭伤。因此，在年度比赛的赛场上，总会停着几辆救护车。

Other Unusual Sports

番茄大战（La Tomatina）

在每年的8月29日，西班牙的工业小镇 Brunol 会举行番茄大战，在那天有约两万名的游客参加了这场食物大战。

棋拳大赛（Chess Boxing）

四肢发达、头脑也不能简单才能赢得棋拳大赛哦！比赛规则是先下三分钟国际象棋，再打三分钟拳击，依次轮回。最后以先将对手下输或击倒的人为胜。

极限熨衣（Extreme Ironing）

是另类极限体育运动。参赛者需带着衣服、熨斗及熨衣板，在悬崖边、雪山、海底等极限条件下熨衣服。

Dog Sledding

Monroe Mann

Last year, I learned how to dog sled. A dog sled is a sled that is pulled through the snow and ice by six to ten sled dogs. These dogs LOVE to pull, and when I gave the command to mush, the dogs were so incredibly excited! The joy that the dogs yelped out during the sled runs was amazing!

狗拉雪橇

去年，我学习了如何训练狗拉雪橇。狗拉雪橇是由6到10只狗拉着雪橇在雪和冰上滑行。这些狗很喜欢拉雪橇，并且当我发出指令“前进”时，狗会异常兴奋！狗的高兴劲儿在雪橇滑行的过程中得到了惊人的释放。

西伯利亚雪橇犬是原始的古老犬种，在西伯利亚东北部、格陵兰南部生活。而它哈士奇（Husky）名字的由来，是源自其独特的嘶哑叫声。西伯利亚雪橇犬有着比大多数犬种都要厚的毛发。它们毛发的颜色和花纹有很多种类。通常有着白色的爪和四肢、面部的花纹和较尖的尾部，最常见的毛色搭配有黑夹白、灰夹白、铜红色（copper-red）夹白和纯白色，很多个体还有褐色、微红色的毛，灰棕色阴影或者杂色斑点。面部出现类似面具、眼镜形状各种各样的花纹也是很常见的。因为基因比其他种类的犬更接近原祖的狼，西伯利亚雪橇犬都有着和狼相似的外观，除了体型较小与较为柔顺的毛发。哈士奇外观帅气独特，性格热情好动还有点内向胆小，爱干净吃得少，现在已经成了风靡网络的红狗哦！

The "All Black's Haka" Story

Lindsey Bard

The international rugby team for New Zealand, the All Blacks, have a tradition. Before each game they perform a war dance called the Haka. It is a chanted song with arm slapping, foot stamping and scary faces. It shows respect for their culture and is meant to scare their opponents. New Zealand has a small population, but one of the best rugby teams in the world. Is the Haka part of the reason why?

黑衫军哈卡舞

新西兰国际橄榄球队黑衫军有一个传统。在开赛前，他们会表演一种叫作哈卡的赛前舞。它是一首吟唱的歌曲，伴随着节奏，人们拍打手臂，并配以跺脚的动作以及震慑的表情。这是向他们（土著）的文化致敬，同时也含有威慑对手的意思。新西兰人口稀少，但却拥有全世界最棒的橄榄球队。而哈卡舞是否就是新西兰球队制胜的秘密武器呢?

Americans Love Football!

Heather Pfeiffer

While in America it's just called football, other countries refer to this beloved sport as American football, and it is no doubt one of the hottest sports in the USA. American football is organized by the NFL (National Football League)which earns multiple billions of dollars annually. This year during the 2013 Superbowl (final game of the football season) 71% of U.S. households watched the game, making it the most-watched television event in history!

美国人热爱橄榄球！

在美国，“football”就是橄榄球，而其他国家把这个备受人喜爱的运动叫作美式橄榄球，它毫无疑问是美国最受欢迎的运动之一。橄榄球是由美国国家美式橄榄球大联盟组织的，这个组织每年收入达几十个亿。在2013年的“超级碗”（赛季的最后一场比赛），71%的美国家庭观看了这个比赛，这使得它成了有史以来收视率最高的电视节目。

Slam Dunk

Heather Pfeiffer

Do you watch the NBA? Do you enjoy playing a game of b-ball yourself every now and again? Can you jump high enough to slam dunk a ball? In basketball, a slam dunk is a forceful move in which the player jumps and tosses the ball into the hoop. A slam dunk may also be used to describe a situation which is certain to succeed.

扣 篮

你看美国篮球职业联赛吗？你喜欢偶尔打打篮球吗？你能跳得够高，然后扣篮吗？在篮球里，扣篮是一个剧烈的动作，运动员跳高并把球扔进篮筐中。扣篮这个词也可以用来描述一种必定成功的形势。

除了扣篮之外，让我们再了解一些与篮球比赛相关的词汇吧！

球场 court
前锋 forwards
后卫 guards
中锋 center
后场 backcourt
前场 frontcourt
组织后卫 point guard
得分后卫 shooting guard
篮筐 rim,basket
争球 jump ball
攻方 offense
守方 defence
计时器 shot clock
打成平分 tie
加时赛 overtime(OT)

运球 dribbling
传球 pass
上篮得分 layup
跳投 jump shot
勾手投篮 hook shot
罚球 foul shot
篮板 rebound
助攻 assists
内线得分 points in paint
暂停 time-out
人盯人 men-to-men defense
区域防守 zone defense
盖帽 blocking
失误 turnovers
常规赛 regular season

Feeling Blue

Garmaan Nq

Do you suffer from stress and anxiety? Are you under pressure from work? Eating right can help reduce stress levels. Blueberries can help improve brain function and energize you naturally. Almonds are rich in vitamins, which help pep you up. Milk, yogurt, eggs and other proteins increase epinephrine* and dopamine* in the brain, which are soothing neurotransmitters*. Fatty fish, like salmon and mackerel,can help everything from your brain to your heart. Oats, soy, poultry and sesame seeds help you relax. Beef and foods rich in vitamin B can help your body regulate brain function.

忧 郁

你在忍受焦虑带来的痛苦吗？工作给你带来压力了吗？正确的饮食能（帮助你）减轻压力。蓝莓可以改善大脑功能，并且天然地为你补给能量。杏仁含有丰富的维生素，它能帮助你振作。牛奶、酸奶、鸡蛋还有其他的蛋白质，能增加大脑的肾上腺素和多巴胺的分泌，舒缓神经。含有脂肪的鱼类，例如三文鱼和马鲛鱼，则好处更多，对大脑和心脏都有益处。燕麦、大豆、家禽以及芝麻，也能帮你放松。牛肉和含有丰富维生素B的食物，能帮助你调节大脑功能。

*epinephrine: 肾上腺素，是一种激素和神经传导物质。

*dopamine: 多巴胺，是一种脑内分泌物，属于神经递质，它的分泌可以影响人的情绪。

*neurotransmitters: 神经递质，凡是神经细胞间神经信息传递中介的化学物质，统称神经递质。

Vitamins and Health Supplements

Allen Mak

Vitamins and health supplements are a billion dollar business. The question is, "Are vitamins and health supplements useful?" Doctors across the world have different opinions and facts about taking vitamins. But one fact I know is that these products continue to increase in emerging markets. So how often do you take vitamins?

维生素和保健品

维生素和保健品做的是十亿美元的生意。问题是"维生素和保健品真的有效果吗？"世界各地的医生，对于服用维生素有着不同的看法和相关的案例。而我知道的一个事实是，这些产品的市场在持续增长。你多久服用一次维生素呢?

Energy Drinks

Allen Mak

How often do you drink energy drinks? Many students nowadays would drink these so that they could study all night long. It should temporarily assist us when we are tired or in need of a boost. The key word here is temporarily, but nowadays it seems that many people drink it constantly, which isn't really what energy drinks were intended for. So, parents should beware of this new trend among students!

能量型饮料

你多久会喝一次能量型饮料呢？现如今，许多学生喝这样的能量型饮料，以帮助他们通宵熬夜学习。它可能能够暂时在我们感到疲惫或者需要补充能量的时候起到作用。关键在于“暂时”二字，现在貌似很多人会选择频繁地喝这种饮料，这显然不是能量型饮料生产的真正用意。因此，父母们应该注意在学生中流行的这种新趋势。

能量型饮料对身体危害大

美国一项研究表明，一些能量型饮料中的咖啡因含量很高。而咖啡因可能与能量型饮料中的其他成分，如牛磺酸、维生素或矿物质发生反应。有时，人们把能量型饮料与酒混在一起喝，这对心率、血压甚至人的精神状态都会有影响。而且，能量型饮料能够令血压升高、心率加快，并且可能导致身体严重脱水。因此，剧烈运动后喝水或含电解质、矿物质以及碳水化合物的运动型饮料应该是更好的选择。

To Feel As Fit As a Fiddle

Garmaan Ng

Not only does what you eat affects your mood and health but so does sleeping enough - you should always try and sleep between seven to eight hours per night. To allow your skin to feel the same get out into the sun. Allow your skin at least twenty minutes a day in the sun. The sun rays are good for your skin and your mood, too.

如何保持最佳的身体状态

不仅你吃的食物会影响你的情绪和健康，睡眠充足与否也会影响。首先是每晚你应该尽量睡足七到八个小时。此外，让肌肤接触阳光。每天至少让你的肌肤在阳光下沐浴20分钟。阳光的照射对皮肤和情绪都有好处。

30-Day Challenges

Heather Pfeiffer

Ever feel like you haven't accomplished much recently? Setting short term goals is an effective way to improve productivity and boost your overall mental health. In order to do this, I urge you to take the 30-day challenge. Personalize your 30-day challenge: tell someone "In 30 days I will...write a story/paint a picture/learn 100 words" . Decide on a goal which is realistic and attainable and do something each day to move towards it. Ready, set, go!

30天挑战

是否觉得最近的你缺乏成就感呢？设定一个短期的目标，是一种提高产出的有效方法，同时，也能全面地改善你的心理健康。为了做到这点，我鼓励你采用“30天挑战法”。个性化设计你的“30天挑战”：告诉别人你将在30天里构思一个故事、画上一幅画或者学习100个单词。由你来决定哪个目标是可实现的和可以达到的，每天朝目标迈进一步。准备，设定目标，然后开始行动吧！

Yoga

Cher Reynolds

Yoga can improve your health in many ways such as flexibility, breathing, posture and strength, and it can even improve your mind. Yoga can give you inner peace and better concentration, and we all need that living a busy city life! There are many different types of yoga, from Vinyasa yoga which is popular in America and has a wide variety of poses, and Hatha yoga which contains slow movements and is great for winding down after a long day, to Bikram Yoga which is usually practiced in 105 degree heat and 40% humidity. Find your own style today and get healthy!

瑜 伽

瑜伽可以多方面提升你的健康状况，例如增强身体的灵活性、调整呼吸、健美体态和提升力量。它甚至能改善你的脑力。瑜伽可以给你带来内心的平静，帮助你更好地集中注意力，那是我们在繁忙的城市生活中所需要的。瑜伽种类很多：比如在美国很流行包含了很多各种各样姿势的流瑜伽；哈达瑜伽主要包括缓慢的运动，它能很好地帮助你在漫长的一天过后舒展身体；高温瑜伽通常是在105度下进行练习，并且湿度需达到40%。找到适合你的瑜伽方式，然后开始变得健康吧！

瑜伽运动的相关词汇

瑜伽 yoga
柔韧度 nimbleness
自控力 self-control
意志力 resistance
瑜伽服 yoga wear
瑜伽垫 yoga mat
热身训练 warm-up
姿势 pose
直角式 right angle pose
牛面式 cow's face pose
吸气 inhale
呼气 exhale
伸直手臂 stretch your arms
前倾 bend forward
伸直膝盖 keep your knees straight
向上看 look upward
仰卧 lie flat on the back
俯卧 lie flat on the stomach
颈旋转 neck rolls
放松 relax
反复 repeat
腿部伸展 leg stretches
肩旋转 shoulder rotation
尽可能地向后看
look back as far as possible
把下巴靠近胸口
drop your chin to your chest

Chapter 5 Fun Idioms 英语趣多多

Sometimes, learning a language becomes much easier when it's simply fun! These idioms are fun to learn, easy to remember and can give you an insight into British and American culture.

有时候，当语言变得好玩的时候学起来会尤其容易。接下来我们选择了一些有趣又好记的英语俚语，通过学习你还能深入了解英美的文化。

Apple of My Eye

Tessa Xioutas

"Apple of my eye" is a common idiom we use in English meaning that a person is very precious and special to you; this person is usually adored by someone. Typically, parents will refer to their children as this.

Daniel: How's your daughter doing?

David: Oh,she's doing great! She's the sweetest baby and the apple of my eye!

我的心中挚爱

"Apple of my eye"是英语中我们常用的一个短语，它所表达的意思是，某人对你而言非常珍贵与特别。这个人通常被别人宠爱。通常，父母们会用这种表达方式来形容自己的孩子。

丹尼尔：你女儿最近怎么样?

大卫：噢，她很棒! 她是我最亲爱的宝贝，我的唯一!

As Cool As a Cucumber

Tessa Xioutas

Are you as cool as a cucumber? This is an idiom meaning that you feel extremely calm. For example, before Janet's big presentation she felt as cool as a cucumber, but her partner felt extremely nervous. This idiom is probably based on the fact that even in hot weather, cucumbers remain cool on the inside. Who is the coolest person you know?

镇定自若

你是个镇定自若的人吗？这是一个用来形容极其镇静的状态的短语。例如，珍妮特在做演讲之前镇定自若，但是她的伙伴十分紧张。这个短语可能是来自于一个自然现象：即使在炎热的气候下，黄瓜的内部仍然保持低温。谁是你见到过的最镇定的人？

Cute As a Button

Rand Herz

There are many ways to describe someone who is attractive or appealing. If something or someone is pretty in a way that makes another happy or joyous, this is cute. It is often used to describe something young or child-like. For some reasons, if something is really cute, we compare it to a button. This is simply an idiom.

"Have you seen Erica's new baby? He's only a few days old!"

"No, but everybody is talking about it. They all say he is just cute as a button."

纽扣般可爱

描述某人很有吸引力或是很有魅力的方式很多。如果某事物或者某人漂亮得让人高兴愉悦，这就是可爱（cute）。“Cute”这个词通常用于描述一些年轻或者像孩子一样的事物。由于一些不知名的原因，如果某物真的很可爱，我们通常将它和纽扣做比较。“cute as a button”就成了一个习语。

“你见过埃里卡的小孩了吗？他才刚出生不久。”

“没有，但是每个人都在谈论他，他们都在说他跟纽扣一样可爱。”

It's Raining Cats and Dogs

Allen Mak

This expression means to rain heavily. Let me give you an example: Today, when I got up my garden and my porch was all wet. My outdoor swimming pool was also half full. Last night, I remember hearing the heavy rain and the thunder. It must have been raining cats and dogs last night while I was sleeping.

倾盆大雨

这是一个用来描述“雨下得很大”的表达。例如：今天，当我来到花园的时候，门廊全都湿了，而我室外的游泳池也都注了一半的水。昨晚，我听到了很大的雨声和雷声，一定是在我睡觉的时候下了倾盆大雨。

She Is so High Maintenance!

Tessa Xioutas

"High maintenance" is an expression used to describe a person who needs a lot of attention in relationships/romantic relationships etc., and can be quite emotionally needy. Usually, this expression is used to describe a female. For example, Joey told his friend: "I think I'm going to end my relationship with Jenny. She wants me to call her every hour! She is so high maintenance!" Do you know anyone who is high maintenance?

她真难伺候!

"High maintenance"用来描述一种人：这种人在人际和感情等关系中需要较多关注，并且有十分强烈的情感需要。这个表达通常用来形容女性。例如，乔伊告诉他的朋友："我快要跟珍妮分手了。她想要我每个小时都打电话给她！她真难伺候！"你知道谁是难伺候的吗?

When Pigs Fly!

Tessa Xioutas

"When pigs fly" is an idiom we use to say that you will never say yes to something that you don't want to do. For example:

Natalie: Will you cook dinner for me?

Krista: When pigs fly! You know I hate cooking!

除非猪会飞（绝不可能）！

"When pigs fly" 是一个俚语，用来表达：你决不会向你不想做的事情说"是"的心情。例如：

纳塔利：你能为我做晚餐吗？

克丽丝塔：除非猪会飞！你知道我讨厌做饭！

To Jump the Shark

Linda Napikoski

The phrase comes from reaction to an episode of the television show *Happy Days*, in which a character jumped over a shark while waterskiing. Viewers thought it was unrealistic and silly. Now, when some popular entertainment is dropping in quality and seems desperate to continue attracting attention, we say it has "jumped the shark". What TV shows can you think of that have jumped the shark?

哗众取宠

这个词的典故出自电视节目《欢乐时光》中的一集，里面的一位主角在滑水的时候跳上了鲨鱼背。收看该节目的观众认为，主角这样的表现显得华而不实而且很愚蠢。如今，一些曾经受欢迎的娱乐节目的水准在往下走，当节目本身已经无法再吸引观众持续的关注时，往往会做出类似“跳上鲨鱼背”的哗众取宠的行为。你觉得哪些电视节目也是通过哗众取宠来博眼球的?

在这几篇文章中，我们都接触到了与动物相关的英语习语，其实在英语中，与动物相关的习语还有很多，下面就向大家介绍几个。

Let sleeping dogs lie.
勿惹是生非。

Never offer to teach fish to swim.
不要班门弄斧。

The best fish swim near the bottom.
好鱼常在水底游。

It's an ill bird that fouls its own nest.
家丑不可外扬。

Fine feathers make fine birds.
人要衣装，马要鞍。

A bird is known by its note, and a man by his talk.
听音识鸟，闻言识人。

He who would hang his dog gives out first that it is mad.
欲加之罪，何患无辞。

A **crow**（乌鸦）is never the whiter for washing herself often.
江山易改，本性难移。

To Bite Off More Than You Can Chew

Allen Mak

Imagine your waiter brings you a huge super-sized hamburger. In your hunger, you grab it quickly and take a giant bite out of it. Unfortunately, the bite you've taken is too big. Now you need to swallow this bite down while drinking water and at the same time trying not to choke. The idiom means the attempt to take on a task that is too much for you to handle.

贪多嚼不烂

想象一下，服务生给你上了一个超大的汉堡，你饥肠辘辘，迅速地拿起它，然后大口咬下去。不幸的是，你咬了太大的一口。现在你不得不喝水才能把这一大口吞下去，并且得小心不噎到自己。以此类推，这个习语的意思是指一个人（不自量力地）尝试揽下超过你自身能力的活儿。

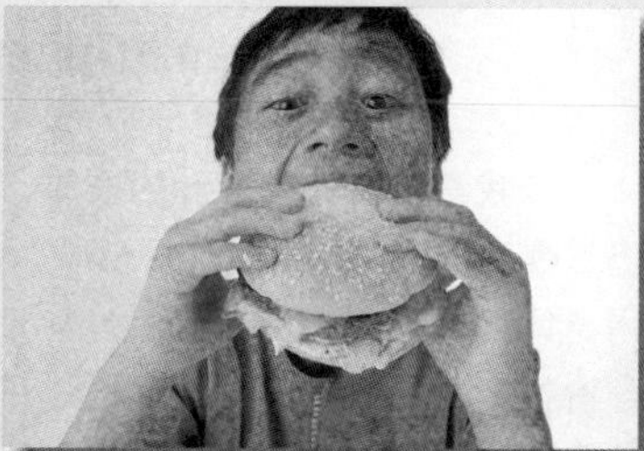

Something Costs an Arm and a Leg

Heather Pfeiffer

"I love designer clothes, but even when they are on sale, they still cost an arm and a leg!" To cost an arm and a leg doesn't mean that you pay in body parts; instead it simply expresses how expensive something is. Have you ever said something similar to this before? Perhaps, if you've ever been in the market for a new house, you know that buying a house costs an arm and a leg! This idiom may be used to describe anything you believe costs a lot of money. Have you bought anything recently that costs an arm and a leg?

昂贵的代价

"我喜欢设计师设计的衣服，但是尽管衣服在打折，仍然很贵！""To cost an arm and a leg"并不是说你要用身体的某个部位作为代价，它只是一个简单的短语，形容价格非常昂贵。你曾经这样说过吗？如果你曾打算购置新居，你就会知道买房子非常昂贵。这个习语可用来描述你认为会花掉你一大笔钱的消费。最近，你有买过什么很昂贵的东西吗？

It's All Greek to Me!

Tessa Xioutas

When I'm studying Chinese I usually feel really confused and think to myself, "It's all Greek to me!" You might be thinking "how could it be Greek, when it's Chinese?" This is an idiom we use to express that the situation or the material is too difficult to understand. Much like if I spoke to you in Greek, you wouldn't have any idea what I was saying or what it means! When I watch football, because I don't understand any of the rules, I can say, "It's all Greek to me!" Perhaps you sometimes feel this way when you're learning English.

一窍不通（如同天书）！

当学习中文的时候，我真的常常感到疑惑并且自己思索着："中文对我而言就是希腊语！"你可能会想，明明在学中文，怎么又扯上希腊语了呢？原来这是一个习语，我们用它来描述难懂的处境或事物。就好比如果我跟你说希腊语，你可能听天书般完全摸不着头脑！比如，当我在看足球赛的时候，因为我不懂得任何规则，我可以说，"It's all greek to me"（我对足球规则一窍不通）！或许你在学英文的时候，偶尔也会有这种感觉。

We're in the Same Boat

Philip Simpson

Learning English can be a challenge, and sometimes students can feel very lonely. When they come to talk to me about their difficulties I will always encourage them to talk to other students after they talk to me, because they will soon discover that many people share their worries, or have experienced their problems. Instead of being alone, they understand that all English students have similar, or shared experiences. "We're in the same boat" means that we are in the same situation, and when it comes to learning English, we are all in the same boat!

我们在同一条船上（我们处境相同）

学习英语有时会是一种挑战，并且学生偶尔会感到学习很孤独。当学生来跟我讲他们学习中遇到的困难时，我总是鼓励他们在和我说完之后，再跟其他学生也说说。明白所有的英语学习者都会有相似的烦恼与经历之后，他们就不会感觉孤独了。我们的处境相同，意思是，我们都处在相同的境地。在英语学习中，我们处境相同。

To Break the Ice

Philip Simpson

When meeting new people in Wall Street classes, students can often be shy, so teachers will design activities at the beginning of the class to help students overcome their shyness, and help them to relax and feel comfortable talking to someone new. Also if you want to talk to that beautiful girl/handsome man you see on the bus you might need to say something to begin the conversation. In these two situations we are trying to break the ice; to make the first move to help people overcome their shyness. Maybe you can try this joke: "How much does a polar bear weigh? Enough to break the ice!"

破 冰

当在华尔街英语课上遇见新同学的时候，学生通常会害羞，因此老师们会在开始上课的时候设计一些教学活动来帮助学生克服羞涩，帮助他们放松，以便他们可以轻松地跟新同学说话。同样，当你想跟在车上看见的漂亮女孩/帅气男孩搭话，你需要说些什么来开始交谈。在这两种情况下，我们尝试破冰，以帮助人们克服害羞，迈出第一步。也许你可以在破冰时尝试和朋友开这样的玩笑：“一头北极熊有多重呢？它重得足够破冰！”

See Eye to Eye

Heather Pfeiffer

We can't see eye to eye on anything! This idiom may seem a bit confusing at first sight, but it simply means to agree. The saying is usually used in sentences similar to this one, i.e. we see eye to eye on this situation or we don't see eye to eye on this matter. We can't see eye to eye means two people are unable to agree with each other.

达成共识

我们不能在任何事情上都达成共识（see eye to eye）！乍看这个短语，可能会令人不解，但其实这个短语所表达的意思很简单，就是“看法一致”。这个说法通常用于类似的句子中，例如：在这种情况下，我们意见一致；或者，我们不能在此事上达成一致。而“We can’t see eye to eye”表示两个人不能同意彼此的意见，无法达成一致。

To Be Neck and Neck

Heather Pfeiffer

After they had launched their new product, the company's stock appreciated which meant they were now finally neck and neck with their long-standing competitor. Think of two people running a race, side by side. No one knows who will win. They are so close that anyone could win. In this case, they are neck and neck. To be neck and neck means that two rivals are at the same level with one another.

并驾齐驱

在他们发布新的产品之后，公司股价随之攀升。这意味着，他们现在终于和长期的竞争对手并驾齐驱。试想两个人的赛跑，肩并着肩，没人知道谁会赢得比赛。他们太接近彼此，以至于都有赢得比赛的可能。这种情况，他们处于“并驾齐驱”的状态。“To be neck and neck”的意思是，两个竞争对手处在同样的水平线上，不分上下。

Scratch Someone's Back

Allen Mak

We all know how difficult it is to scratch that itch on your back. So we need someone else do it for you, but in return you'll probably need to scratch that person's itch on his/her back. This is quite an important idiom to learn because we all learn that if you do someone a favor then that person would return a favor.

替人挠背（这回你帮我，下回我帮你）

我们都知道，挠背上的痒很困难。因此，我们需要别人帮忙挠背上的痒。但是作为报答，你也要给那个帮你的人挠痒。“Scratch someone's back” 是相当重要的短语，因为我们都知道，如果你帮了某人的忙，那么之后那个人要回报你给予的恩惠。

Keep One's Eye on the Ball

Heather Pfeiffer

If the coach shouts "Keep your eye on the ball", it means the person is not following the game closely. Distraction or negligence may have caused the player to make a mistake. To keep your eye on the ball means to stay alert and keep your mind on the task at hand. This phrase can also be used in other situations unrelated to sports if someone loses focus on their particular goal or target. For example, the meeting started to get off topic when one team member brought up last night's dinner. The director asked everyone politely, "Can we all just keep our eyes on the ball and get back to the point of the meeting?"

集中精力

如果教练大叫着说："keep your eye on the ball." 意思是，这个人在运动时注意力不集中。而注意力涣散或粗心大意会导致运动员犯错。"keep your eye on the ball" 的意思是，保持警惕性并且把心思放在当前的任务上。这个短语同样可以用在失去特定目标和焦点的其他非体育运动的场景中。例如，在会议上，当队友提及昨晚晚餐的题外话时，总监礼貌地提醒大家说："我们能集中精力回到这次会议的重点上来吗？"

Cloud Nine

Tessa Xioutas

My friend's boyfriend took her to Italy and proposed to her! She felt extremely happy and said that she felt like she was on "cloud nine" !We can use this idiom to express that we're extremely happy. Another friend was sad over a break-up. I told her that "every cloud has a silver lining". We use this idiom when we want to express optimism: dark times lead to bright days! When she began dating a new guy, not only did she feel like she was on "cloud nine" ,but she also realized that "every cloud has a silver lining" .

乐上九霄云外

我朋友的男朋友带她去意大利并向她求婚了！她感到无比得快乐，并说感觉简直像飞到了九霄云外！我们可以用这个习语来表达我们非常开心。另一个朋友由于分手而伤心。我告诉她："困境中总有会有一丝光明（every cloud has a silver lining）。"当我们想要表达积极乐观的意思时，会使用这个习语：黑暗是通往光明之路！当她开始跟新的男生约会时，她会飞到九霄云外般的开心，同时她也看到了"乌云背后的幸福线"。

Chin Up

Heather Pfeiffer

Hey, chin up! This is a great way to tell your friends to try to look at the bright side. Just as it sounds, chin up just means that you should lift your head in light of your worries, sorrows, etc. and think about something positive. This is usually said to give advice or consolation to someone who is feeling down.

抬起下巴（振奋起来）

嗨，振作起来！这是一个告诉朋友往好处想的好方法。正如字面意思一样，“chin up”的意思就是抬起下巴，从担心、悲伤等情绪中振作起来，学会正面思考。常常在给情绪低落的人建议或者安抚时会用到这个短语。

Between a Rock and a Hard Place

Allen Mak

Have you ever heard of this saying, "between a rock and a hard place"? We usually use this to describe a dilemma, which someone may have. An example is if your mother and your wife got into an argument whose side would you take? You'll be stuck with a dilemma because there are no good choices. That is why we say you are stuck between a rock and a hard place because you have nowhere to go.

进退两难

你曾听过“between a rock and a hard place（进退两难）”这样的说法吗？我们通常使用这个短语来描述一个人可能所处的两难境遇。例如，如果你的妈妈和你的妻子发生了争执，你会选择站在哪一边呢？你可能会陷入两难的境地，因为原本就没有更好的选择。所以我们会说“you are stuck between a rock and a hard place”，因为此时的你处在两难的境地，根本无从抉择。

Break a Leg

Lindsey Bard

As the actress was ready to step on stage, someone whispered, "Break a leg", the traditional wish for good luck. Traditionally, spirits live in theaters and if you wish someone "good luck" the spirits will do something bad. The broken legs were to trick the spirits into doing good.

祝你好运的故事

女演员准备上台，有人低声说着"break a leg"，这是传统的祈求好运的方式。传说，幽灵住在剧院里，如果你祝某人"good luck（好运）"，这些幽灵就会出来作祟。而说反语跌断腿倒不失为引诱幽灵做好事的一种方法。

To Have One's Hands Full

Lindsey Bard

As we prepare for Chinese New Year it is easy to "have one's hands full". With so many things to finish and do we might feel we have more than we can manage and we can't do any more. Our schedule and hands are full.

忙得不可开交

当我们在为中国的新年做准备的时候，很容易会让人“忙得不可开交”。许多事等待完成，我们可能感到事情远比我们所能应付的要多，令人难以招架。我们的计划和手上的事情都满满当当。

Hop On, Hop Off!

Tessa Xioutas

A London hop-on, hop-off (get off, get on) tour bus is a fantastic way to see the city and all of its popular sights at your own speed. From major attractions like The London Eye to Buckingham Palace, the regular buses, equipped with headsets in various languages, will bring you to your desired location. This also includes a river cruise on the Thames. What are you waiting for?

上车，下车

在伦敦乘坐旅游观光巴士不失为一种非常棒的游览整座城市的方式。你可以按照自己的节奏去游览所有热门景点。在那些最著名的景点，比如从伦敦眼到白金汉宫，都有观光巴士定时靠站停靠。车上配备耳麦，提供各种语言的讲解，会带你去任何你想去的地方。同样，在泰晤士河上还有观光游览船。你还在等什么呢？

Kill It

Heather Pfeiffer

You are eating dinner with your friends and have almost eaten all of the food, but there's still one slice of pizza left. You friend, who is already full, turns toward you and tells you: "kill it." What do they mean? Kill the pizza? How? Answer: just eat it. When there's only a small amount of food or drink left, "kill it" means to finish the food. So next time you're eating with your friends and you are almost finished, tell them to kill it.

吃光它

你正在和朋友吃晚餐，你们俩几乎把所有的食物都吃完了，只剩下一小片披萨。可是你的朋友已经吃饱了，他（她）转过头来告诉你："杀死它（kill it的字面意思）。"他（她）要表达什么意思呢？杀死披萨？怎么杀？答案是：直接吃光。当只有一点食物或者饮料剩下的时候，"kill it"的意思是吃完剩下的食物。因此，下次你和朋友吃饭，等到快吃完了的时候，告诉他们"kill it"，把剩下的吃光。

Tie the Knot

Tessa Xioutas

Have you ever tied the knot? This is an idiom used to describe two people who will get married. For example, my sister recently got married; so, now I can say that she "tied the knot"!

Kristina: When will you tie the knot?

Andrea: I'm tying the knot next week!

喜结连理

你尝试过系结吗？"Tie the knot"这个短语用来表达两个人结婚。例如，我的姐姐最近结婚了；因此，我现在可以说她"tied the knot（喜结连理）"！

克里斯汀娜："你什么时候结婚呢？"

安德丽亚："我下个礼拜就要结婚了！"

Fall Behind

Heather Pfeiffer

I was so busy with work this week that I fell behind with my studies. To fall behind means that you go slower than or fail to keep up with a class, a group or deadlines. For example, I wanted to finish the report by this week, but since my daughter was sick I fell behind schedule. Imagine your rent was due last week and you still haven't paid it. In this case, how can you describe this situation using fall behind?

落　后

这个礼拜工作太忙了，我的学习都跟不上了。“To fall behind”意思是你的进度跟同班、同组或者跟某截止日期相比变慢了，跟不上。例如，我想这个礼拜完成报告，但是自从我女儿生病，我的进度就落后了。设想你的房租上礼拜到期，但是你至今仍然没付。在这种情况下，你怎么使用“fall behind（到期）”来描述这样的情景呢?

Procrastination（拖延症）is a popular word on the Internet. It is used to describe the practice of **carrying out**（执行）**less urgent**（不紧急的）tasks **in preference to**（优先于）more urgent ones, or doing more **pleasurable**（令人愉快的）things **in place of**（代替）less pleasurable ones, and thus **putting off**（推迟）**impending**（紧急的）tasks to a later time, sometimes to the "last minute" before the **deadline**（最后期限）.

Compare Apples to Oranges

Heather Pfeiffer

Surely, I like Zhao Benshan and enjoy watching Zhang Ziyi, but comparing these actors is like comparing apples to oranges. They are completely different - different movies, different styles, different gender, etc. There's no way I could choose which one is better, because I like them for different reasons. To compare apples to oranges means to compare two unlike things.

苹果和橘子无法相提并论

毫无疑问，我喜欢赵本山，同时也喜欢看章子怡在大银幕上的表演，但是比较这两位演员就如同在比较苹果和橘子。他们完全不一样，没有任何可比性 ——不同的电影、不同的风格、不同的性别，等等。我完全不能说他们中的某一个比另一个更好，因为我喜欢他们的原因各不相同。把“苹果与橘子放在一起做比较”的意思是：把两个完全不同的事物进行比较。

Dog-eat-dog

Heather Pfeiffer

Big cities are all dog-eat-dog. Why? Because everyone is looking out for their own interests and how to better themselves, even if others lose in the process. That's the idea of competition. Is it possible to sustain growth and competition without stepping all over each other?

你死我活的竞争（狗咬狗）

大城市里的竞争如同狗咬狗那般残酷激烈。为什么？因为每个人都为了追逐自身的利益，想让自己过得更好，哪怕在追逐的过程中有人惨遭失败——这就是竞争的本质。有没有可能做到保证个人持续发展的同时，保持一种（良性）竞争，避免践踏他人的利益呢？

Grandfathered In

Heather Pfeiffer

In the 1st season of the American TV series *Prison Break*, an old, prisoner named Westmoreland is introduced along with his gray cat. Cats are not allowed at the prison, but they used to be permitted (as companions for the prisoners). Therefore, the cat was grandfathered in. If something is grandfathered in, it means that the old rule applies to those who were already granted permission before the regulation changed, but for all future cases, everyone else must abide by the new law.

授予特权

在美国电视剧《越狱》第一季中，一位年老的、叫作维斯特摩兰的罪犯，他和他的灰色猫咪一同出场。如今的监狱里不允许养猫，但是过去的法律允许（猫可以给囚犯做伴）。因此，猫被“授予特权（grandfathered in）”可以待在监狱里。如果某种行为被授予特权而被允许存在，那意味着旧的规则对于在新条款出台前的那些人依然适用，即这群人可以享有特权依旧遵循旧的规则。但是对所有在新条款生效后发生的事，则必须遵守新的法律。

Chapter 6 Metropolitan Life 大都市生活

In the modern world, life is very different for us than it was for our ancestors. Some of these changes are exciting, some are challenging, and some are unimportant but fun to have. Read on, and decide which ones are which!

现代社会，我们的生活与我们祖先的生活相比已经有了翻天覆地的变化。有些变化令人激动，有些变化富于挑战，有些变化可能无关紧要但人们倒也乐意接受。读读本章，告诉我们这些变化给你带来的感受！

Starting Your Day Off on the Right Foot

Heather Pfeiffer

It's another Monday. The sound of your alarm rings, you are painfully trying to pull yourself out of bed. How about a different way of starting your day? Try starting your day off on the right foot (in other words, to begin your day with a good start) by adding these ideas to your morning routine: twenty minutes of relaxation time to listen to music or read the newspaper while eating breakfast; this creates a healthier balance of personal time and work time, rather than beginning your day off with obligatory tasks. Stretch your body. Move one arm across your chest, touch your toes and raise your arms. This will not only help wake you up but improve your general health by increasing blood flow and therefore, oxygen throughout your body. Open your curtains: bringing natural light into your morning helps release adrenaline that works to wake you up.

正确开始你的一天

又是一个星期一。闹钟响了，你痛苦地把自己从床上拉起来。要以怎样不同的方式开始这一天呢？不妨尝试迈出全新一天的第一步，从为每天早上的例行安排增添些乐趣开始吧：20分钟放松听音乐，或者在吃早餐的时候读会儿报。这样会创造一个私人和工作时间的平衡，而不是例行公事地开始一天。伸展你的身体吧。将一只手臂绕过你的胸前，再用手摸摸你的脚趾头，然后伸展你的手臂。这不仅能帮助你清醒，还能加快你的血液循环，让氧气输送到全身，从而提高你的身体素质。拉开窗帘：让早上的自然光进来，帮助身体释放肾上腺素，它能起到让你清醒的作用。

Road Rage

Allen Mak

Do you drive? Do you get angry when you drive? Do you curse and want to hurt others when you drive? If you answered "yes" to all three of the questions above, then you might have road rage. Road rage is very dangerous medical condition because you won't be able to control your emotion or even your actions. People with road rage will intentionally cause accidents and even get into fights with other drivers. In the U.S., vehicle accidents and deaths are caused by road rage every year. In China, more people are buying cars and the roads are getting more congested. The result of these two conditions will only amount to more road rage. If you do have road rage, it is important to stop driving and start taking public transportation. You can not only save gas money, but also help the environment.

公路暴怒症

你开车吗？当你开车的时候你会生气吗？当你开车的时候，你会诅咒并想要伤害他人吗？如果你对以上三个问题的回答都是“是”，那你可能患有公路暴怒症（road rage）。公路暴怒症是非常危险的健康状况（medical condition），因为你不能控制你的情绪、甚至你的行为。有公路暴怒症的人，会有意引起交通事故，甚至会和其他司机打架。在美国，每年都会有因公路暴怒症引起的交通事故和死亡。在中国，越来越多的人买车，道路也因此变得更拥堵。开车的人越多、道路越拥堵的结果就是引起更多的公路暴怒症。如果你真的有公路暴怒症，最好停止开车，而开始乘坐公共交通。你不仅省了汽油钱，还帮助保护环境。

Safety Seats & Belt

Garmaan Ng

These are now standard in every car throughout the world, in the drivers' seat, passenger seat and all back seats. Plus it is a legal requirement that all people travelling in a car to buckle up. In cars with babies or young children, baby car seats and child seats are required by law. In England if you travel in a taxi with a child or baby either the taxi company has to be notified about the child to accommodate the needs or the parents have to provide one themselves. Not buckling up children in cars is known as reckless endangerment and fines are placed on drivers.

安全座椅和安全带

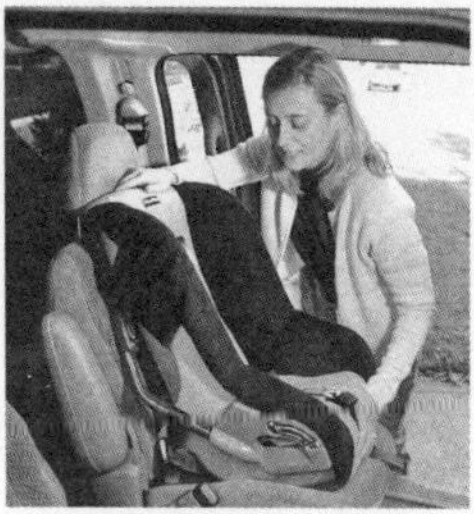

如今，不管是驾驶座、客座还是车后排的所有座位，世界各国车内的座椅都有统一的标准。除此之外，所有的乘车人都被要求在乘车时系紧安全带。载有幼儿或者小孩的车辆，根据法律要求，都需要安装婴儿座椅和儿童座椅。在英格兰，如果你带小孩或者婴儿乘坐出租车外出，出租车公司须注意安排小孩的座位，或者父母自己必须提供相关的座椅设施。车内的小孩不系安全带被视为怠忽致危罪，驾驶员还会因此遭受处罚。

Sanitization Education

Allen Mak

Everyday I've been hearing and reading the news about the Ebola outbreak in Africa. I believe that the key to stopping most infectious diseases is educating people on proper sanitization. Examples: wash your hands daily, cover your mouth if you sneeze, and etc. As my doctor always says we must treat the cause not the symptom.

卫生教育

每天我都听到和看到关于非洲埃博拉疫情暴发的消息。我认为，阻止如此严重传染病的关键在于教授人们正确的卫生知识。例如：每天勤洗手，打喷嚏的时候遮住鼻口，等等。正如我的医生常说的，我们应该预防胜于治疗，防患于未然。

End of the Landline

Allen Mak

A friend recently asked me whether or not he should cancel his landline. Naturally, I said yes because everyone I know uses their mobile phones nowadays. Also some developing countries in Africa are skipping installation of landlines and going straight to cellular service. So maybe in the future we'll only be able to find landline service in the museum.

固定电话的终结

一个朋友最近问我，他是否应该取消固定电话（座机）的业务。我自然十分赞同，因为现在几乎我认识的每个人都在使用手机。同时非洲一些发展中国家正尝试跳过安装座机而直接提供手机通信服务。因此在将来，我们恐怕只能在博物馆里找到固定电话的身影了。

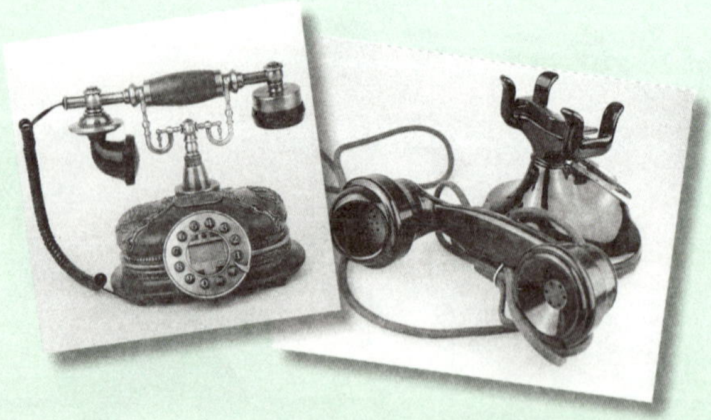

Dangerous Mobile Phones

Garmaan Ng

Most car accident deaths for pedestrians are, walking across roads using their mobile phones with earphones on. Remember while on your phone your focus is taken off the roads. In the western countries it is illegal for any vehicle road users to use their phones without using hands free. This means cyclists, electric scooters, motorcyclists, cars, trucks and bus drivers are prohibited to use their mobile phones in a moving vehicle. It is one of the biggest distractions and can cause serious accidents and death to others. Penalties in these countries are severe.

危险的移动电话

许多车祸发生的原因是行人在过马路的时候戴着耳机打电话。记住，当你在使用电话时，你的注意力被分散了，不再留心马路上的状况。在西方国家，任何在车道上使用手机不开免提是违法的。这同样意味着自行车、电动车、摩托车、汽车、卡车以及公交车的驾驶人员不能在移动交通工具上使用他们的手机。这是一种极为扰乱注意力，并可能导致严重车祸以及他人死亡的行为。西方国家对此行为严惩不贷。

Microphone Hog

Philip Simpson

The next time when you make a plan to go singing in a KTV think carefully about who you invite. In every friendship group there lays a hidden danger, a monster that wakes up when Lady Gaga begins to play. This monster has the power to turn any trip to KTV into a nightmare, and can make old friends hate each other. Of course I am talking about the "microphone hog". To hog something means to keep it to yourself, or be unwilling to share something with others. We can hog many things, food, time, attention, etc. The microphone hog is always singing, changing the order of the songs selected so his/her song arrives faster, and taking the opportunity to sing away from others. Look around your friends, can you identify the microphone hog? If the answer is no, maybe it is you!

麦 霸

下次计划去KTV唱歌时，好好想想你要邀请谁吧！每个朋友圈子都有其潜在的危机，一个怪兽会在点Lady Gaga的歌时苏醒过来。这个怪兽具有将任何一次KTV之旅变成一场噩梦的威力，并且能让老朋友恨上对方。这就是我要说的麦霸（microphone hog）。“To hog something”意思是把东西占为己有或者不愿意跟别人分享。我们可以占有很多东西：食物、时间、关注，等等。麦霸总是在唱歌，改变已选歌的顺序，这样他（她）的歌可以快速提前，然后乘机连续唱歌。看看你周围的朋友，你能找出谁是麦霸吗？如果答案是“否”的话，那么麦霸可能就是你自己哦！

Popular Board Games

Allen Mak

In America, one of our favorite activities is to play board games. Some popular board games are Monopoly and Scrabble. Board games are fun and also a good way for parents to spend time with their children. It's a win-win situation for the whole family. Spend time with your family while having fun!

受欢迎的桌游

在美国，我们非常喜欢的活动之一就是玩桌游。受欢迎的桌游有大富翁以及拼字游戏。桌游非常有趣，同样也是父母与小孩消磨时间的一种方式。对所有家庭成员来说，它算是一项人见人爱的活动！花上一些时间跟你的家人玩桌游，尽情享受其中的乐趣吧！

The Circus

Tessa Xioutas

The Circus is a captivating place for adults and children. It's composed of a group of performers that usually includes a clown, acrobats, animals, jugglers, tight-rope walkers and tigers jumping through flaming hoops! A circus is usually held in a large stadium hosted by a "Ringmaster". Have you ever been to the Circus?

马戏团

马戏团是一个对成人和小孩来说都很迷人的地方。它由一组表演者组成，通常包括小丑、杂技演员、动物、变戏法的人、走钢丝的杂技演员还有跳火圈的老虎。马戏表演通常在大型的运动场馆内进行演出，由一位马戏团领班担任主持。你曾经去看过马戏团表演吗?

Weekend Getaway

Rand Herz

In the busy city lives of today's urban dwellers, it's difficult to find extra time to get away for holiday. Young professionals and middle-aged corporate executives are working hard, focused on getting ahead.

However, it's common to take a weekend adventure, or a weekend getaway. Some people try to do this every weekend. It's a great way to relieve stress and get out into nature. Common activities include spa retreats, camping, hikes and backpacking trips, or short tourist trips to smaller cities. It's easy to do if you leave on Friday as early as possible. You can get to your destination on Friday evening and have two full days of relaxing outside of the city. Some people come back on Sunday evening. Some people push it to Monday morning and come back to go straight to the office. Would you dare to do this?

周末躲清静

如今生活在繁忙都市里的城市居民可能很难有空闲度假。年轻的职业人和中年公司高管都一直埋头苦干，时刻准备向前冲。

然而，周末放个小假或是在周末躲个清静也是很普遍的。有些人每周末都想方设法度一个短假。这是一个很好的减压和亲近大自然的方式。通常，这样的周末活动包括水疗、露营、徒步旅行、背包旅行或者到小城市的短途旅行。人们一般在星期五出发，越早越好。你可以在星期五的傍晚到达你的目的地，然后，在接下来的两天里远离城市，放松自己。有些人会在星期天晚上回来。有些人则将回程时间推迟至星期一的早上，回来后直接去公司上班。你敢这样做吗?

Wanderlust

Philip Simpson

Are you tired of seeing the same street every day? Do you feel like running away from the office to go and see somewhere new? If you answered yes to either of those questions, you might have wanderlust. This isn't actually an English word, but instead a German word that we borrowed/stole! Wanderlust describes a strong feeling to wander or travel around. Most people feel this from time to time, feeling that they need to see something new, while others feel this way all the time, and only work until they have saved enough money to go travelling again!

旅游癖

每天见到相同的街道你会感到厌倦吗？你有没有想过逃离办公室去看看不一样的新事物？如果你对上述两个问题中任何一个的回答是“是”，那你可能就有旅行癖。这实际上不是一个英语词汇，而是从德语借（偷）过来的词！旅行癖用来形容一种很强烈地想要到处走走或者旅行的感觉。因为想见一些新鲜事物，大部分的人时不时都会有这样的感觉，还有些人一直都有这种感觉，而唯一的解决途径就是埋头苦干直到存下足够的钱去进行下一次旅行！

Hotels and Motels

Tessa Xioutas

There are different types of accommodations when you travel. For example, you might want a luxurious experience and stay in a five-star hotel or less expensive choice and choose a motel. If you're on a strict budget, you might opt for a hostel, or a guesthouse. If you enjoy nature, you might go camping and sleep in a tent. If you want a real cultural experience, you might do a "home stay" with a family. Your choice will most likely depend on budget and preference. For example, I'd rather stay in a hotel than a hostel! Where would you rather stay?

酒店和汽车旅馆

旅行的时候，你可以选择不同的住宿方式。例如，如果想要住得比较讲究的话，可以选择住五星级酒店；如果讲究经济实惠的话，就选择汽车旅馆。如果你的预算不多，你可以选择青年旅社或者招待所。如果你喜欢大自然，你可以去露营或睡在帐篷里。如果你想要一种真正的文化体验，你可以选择“寄宿”在当地家庭。你的选择主要取决于你的预算和喜好。例如，我宁愿待在酒店而非青年旅社里！你愿意待在哪儿呢?

Happy Hour

Tessa Xioutas

Happy Hour is a period of time in which hotel, bars, pubs, clubs and restaurants offer a discount price on drinks and food. Happy Hour lasts anywhere between 5-8pm; it typically targets individuals who have finished work for the day. This is popular in western countries; people can take advantage of a good price to eat and drink with friends and co-workers. Have you ever been to Happy Hour?

欢乐时段

“欢乐时段”是酒店、酒吧、酒馆、俱乐部以及餐馆提供折扣价格的食物和饮料的时段。欢乐时段通常从下午五点持续到晚上八点。时段的目标人群是那些结束一天工作的人们。这在西方国家是一个很受欢迎的活动。人们可以借着优惠的价格跟朋友和同事一起吃东西，喝饮料。你享受过欢乐时段吗?

Mix Tapes

Philip Simpson

Long, long ago there was a world with no Internet, and no iPods. In this ancient time, people listened to music on CDs, or before that cassette tapes. People listened to the radio and recorded their favorite songs to make their perfect collection of songs. Sometimes they put together some special love songs and gave them to girls. These home-made albums were called mix tapes, because unlike the ones you bought in a shop they usually had a mix of different artists. Now we use MP3 players we can still use this word, as well as or the more modern "playlist".

自制音乐集锦

很久以前，这个世界上没有网络和iPod（苹果随身播放器）。人们通过播放CD或者更早之前是通过播放磁带听音乐。人们收听收音机时，会把喜欢的歌曲录下来制成自己的歌曲集锦。有时。他们把一些很特别的爱情歌曲录下来放在一起，并把它们送给女孩子。这种家里自制的专辑叫作"mix tapes"。因为不像在商店里买的，它们通常是收集了不同音乐家作品的音乐集锦。现在我们用MP3播放器，仍然可以使用这个词，或者可以用更为现代的说法即"播放曲目列表"。

Rent a Partner.com

Allen Mak

Spring Festival is coming and parents are once again asking that important question, "Have you found a partner yet?" But many parents fail to realize that it isn't easy to find a partner in today's society because our expectations have risen and we have a higher expectation than previous generations. So some people have turned to rental agencies. They are not renting cars, but renting a pretend partner to decrease the amount of pressure from parents. It is a trend and it is likely to continue to grow. Would you ever do this?

租对象网站

春节来临，父母要再次问到那个至关重要的问题：“你找到对象了吗？”但是，许多父母并没有发现，在如今的社会很难找到对象。因为和我们的前辈们相比，我们对于另一半的期望值变得更高。因此一些人不得不求助于租赁中介。他们不是去租车，而是去租一个对象（带回家），以缓解来自父母的压力。这种现象正在成为一种趋势，并且愈演愈烈。你会这样做吗?

相亲（Blind Date）中的谎言

相亲现在已经成为大城市中的单身男女生活中必不可少的一部分。在相亲时，经常要使用一些“客套话”（courtesy）。根据一项对相亲男女的调查，以下几句话是最不可信的，如果在相亲时，你听到下面几句话时，可要当心了哦！

● 以后再联系！（Let's keep in touch !）

三分之一的受访者表示，当他们不想与相亲对象交往时，通常会说这句。

● 这是我第一次相亲。（This is my first time on a blind date.）

受访相亲男性认为女相亲对象的这句话是最不可信的。

● 我不在乎女人的外貌。（I do not care about a woman's appearance.）

受访相亲女性认为男相亲对象的这句话是最不可信的。

● 你给我的印象不错。（You gave me a good impression.）

这句话在男女相亲“最常说的谎言榜”中均位列第四。

Volunteers

Lindsey Bard

Every year millions of people spend time doing jobs they don't get paid for. They receive nothing but smiles and "thank you" from those they help. These people are called "volunteers". They work in hospitals, at parks and libraries, and in the homes of neighbors because they are needed. Do you know anyone who gives to society like this?

志愿者

每年，成千上万的人会用个人时间无偿为他人做事。获得帮助的人回报他们以微笑和感谢，除此之外没有其他的（物质上的）回馈。这些人被称作志愿者。他们在医院、公园、图书馆等地做义工或者到需要他们帮助的邻居家里为他们提供志愿服务。在你的身边有做义工的朋友吗？

南京的志愿服务

素来有着博爱之都美誉的南京的志愿服务活动开展得比较早，有很好的群众基础。目前，全市注册志愿者达140.65万人，占常住人口比重达17.05%。2014年8月28日，举世瞩目的第二届世界青年奥林匹克运动会在南京圆满闭幕。南京广大市民赛前赛后、赛场内外，广泛参与“迎青奥、讲文明、树新风”的志愿服务，百万志愿者以真诚的微笑和热情的服务迎接国内外各方宾客，用自己的实际行动弘扬中华传统美德和“奉献、友爱、互助、进步”的志愿精神，展示了南京人讲文明、重礼仪、团结友善的良好风尚，打造了最美“中国名片”。

Selfies

Allen Mak

Let's take a selfie! This is a new word that was added to the *Oxford English Dictionary in* 2013. It means taking a self-portrait photograph with a handheld mobile device. This was very popular in the US last year with President Obama taking a selfie at a funeral. The trend for selfies actually started in Asia but has now spread around the world. Do you often take selfies?

自 拍

让我们来自拍吧！“Selfies”是一个在2013年被收入《牛津英语字典》里的新词汇。它的意思是通过手持移动设备来给自己拍照。自拍在美国非常流行，就连总统奥巴马也会在葬礼上自拍。“自拍风”实际上源自亚洲，如今已经风靡全球。你会经常自拍吗?

Urbanization and Its Effect

Allen Mak

Urbanization continues to increase globally. This is a trend that will continue in the years to come. Urbanization creates mega cities, and with it comes mega (big) social problems. One main social problem is that people in these cities distrust each other. People become cold and don't help one another. I truly hope that everyone can get along with another. That is my hope for urbanization.

城市化和其带来的影响

全球城市化趋势在持续增长。这种趋势在接下来的几年里会继续下去。城市化创造出超级大都市，并且由此产生很大的社会问题。一个主要的社会问题就是生活在这些超级大都市里的人们不再信任彼此。人们变得冷漠并且不再互相帮助。我真诚地希望，每个人都能跟他人和睦相处。这是我对城市化的期望。

The Art of Saying "No"

Allen Mak

Do you have trouble saying "No" to people? Usually people are afraid to say no because they aren't prepared to say it. When you walk into a situation where you know someone will be asking you for something, you must always prepare the excuse beforehand. Keep a few excuses in your pocket for common requests and use it when necessary.

说“不”的艺术

你是否会觉得和别人说“不”不太容易？通常人们害怕说不，因为他们没准备好说这个词。所以当你能够预见到别人可能会向你索求的时候，你一定要提前准备好应对预案。提前准备好一些应付常见请求的说辞，然后在适当的时候使用。

The 7 Habits of Highly Effective People

Linda Napikoski

Stephen R. Covey's bestselling book *The 7 Habits of Highly Effective People* has inspired businesspeople, world leaders, self-helpers, and millions of other readers around the world. The habits focus on independence, interdependence, and continuous improvement. Among the habits are "Be proactive", "Synergize", and "Think win-win".

高效能人士的七大习惯

史蒂芬·R.柯维的畅销书《高效能人士的七大习惯》鼓舞了商人、世界领袖、自力更生的人，以及世界上数以百万计的读者。这些习惯注重独立、互相依赖以及持续改进，并包括“主动”“协同”以及“双赢”的思维。

The Secret to Life

Heather Pfeiffer

In his book *Blue Zones* Dan Buettner, along with a handful of researchers took a more in-depth look at the diet, lifestyle and environment of communities with some of the oldest people in world. He refers to these areas as "blue zones". What he found was five major similarities: close-knit communities, daily exercise, social engagement and a plant-based/legume diet.

These people who lived to 100 were living in communities where they were not only a valued member of society, but also acted in some way to contribute to the society. Also, many were either vegetarian or mostly vegetarian, sometimes from their own gardens, along with plenty of legumes (peanuts, soybeans, etc.). These elderly folks all had physical activity as a natural part of their daily lives through walking, riding bicycles and so on.

Perhaps, there is something to learn from their healthy habits!

生活的秘密

在丹·比特纳《去最幸福的四国找幸福》的书中，一组调查人员对世界上一些长寿人士的饮食、生活方式以及生活的环境进行了深入的研究。丹·比特纳把这些方面叫作“蓝色地带”。他发现了长寿老人在这些方面五大主要的相似性：密织的社区、每天锻炼身体、参与社会活动，以及以植物豆类为基础的饮食。

百岁老人在他们所住的社区不仅是有价值的社区成员，而且他们也都曾经以某些方式为这个社会做过贡献。许多人是素食主义者或以素食为主，他们吃的植物有时产自他们自己的花园，此外花园里还种了豆类植物（花生、大豆，等等）。这些老年人都把运动自然而然地融入自己的生活当中，比如他们会通过徒步走、骑自行车等健身方式进行锻炼。

或许，我们可以从他们健康的生活习惯中学习到一些东西。

The Secret of Happiness

Absence of occupation is not rest, a mind quite vacant is a mind distressed.

By William Cowper

无所事事不是休息，十分空虚的心灵是痛苦的心灵。

——考伯·W.

All the blessings we enjoy are the fruits of labor, toil, and self-denial, and study.

By Willian Graham Sumner

我们得到的一切幸福都是劳动、辛苦、自我克制和学习的成果。

——萨姆纳·W.G.

Most folks are about as happy as they make up their minds to be.

By Abraham Lincoln

对于大多数人来说，他们认定自己有多幸福，就有多幸福。

——林肯·A.

We have no more right to consume happiness without producing it than to consume wealth without producing it.

By George Bernard Shaw

正像我们无权只享受财富而不创造财富一样，我们也无权只享受幸福而不创造幸福。

——萧伯纳·G.

哈佛大学公开课 “幸福课”的观看网址：http://v.163.com/special/positivepsychology/.